An effective 90-day marketing tool.

market

Sherry Prescott-Willis

th!s

MORGAN JAMES PUBLISHING • NEW YORK

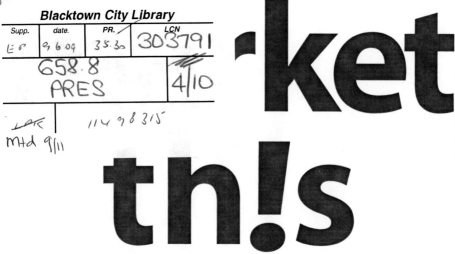

Copyright ©2009 Sherry Prescott-Willis

ISBN: 978-1-60037-497-5 (Paperback)

Library of Congress Control Number: 2008934122

Published by:

MORGAN · JAMES
THE ENTREPRENEURIAL PUBLISHER™
www.morganjamespublishing.com

Morgan James Publishing, LLC
1225 Franklin Ave Suite 325
Garden City, NY 11530-1693
Toll Free 800-485-4943
www.MorganJamesPublishing.com

Cover Illustration by:
Jay Ferracane

Interior Design by:
Rachel Lopez
rachel@r2cdesign.com

Habitat
for Humanity®
Peninsula
Building Partner

THIS BOOK IS DEDICATED TO anyone who has ever believed in marketing something...and to those in my loving family who always believe in me: husband Tom, son Alan, Mom and Dad.

Acknowledgements

SPECIAL THANKS TO: Pete Karagiannis, Lisa Orrell, Susan Monroe, Betsy Burroughs, Carol Iverson, Jon Iverson, Mitchell Levy, Evelyn Preston, Alex Kim, Sheamus Clark, Sandra Shepard, Paula Chang, Dr. Patricia Ross, David Hancock, and Rajas Saxena for your support, enthusiasm, and belief in the message of this book. By trying these exercises on your businesses and by offering constructive feedback, you have helped anneal the processes in a way that I could have not done alone. Many of you tried these exercises on your businesses. Your tireless energy and effort to return constructive feedback has been invaluable! Most importantly, thanks to son Alan for sleeping through so many nights and thanks also to my husband Tom—when Alan did not—without you two being you, this book would not be.

Table of Contents

PART I

Introduction — Evaluating Your Business

IN THIS PART, YOU WILL LEARN why evaluating your business before you do a marketing plan is so important. You will also be introduced to how this book is set up and learn how you can use it to maximize success in your own business. Next you will find an overview and definition of marketing and business plans and learn why and how companies use them.

Introduction

Congratulations! I'm excited for you because you've picked up my book, and you are interested in becoming a savvy marketer. You want to market something, and you want to do it right. This means you have a business or are part of a business and you have a product or service about which you want to get the word out. You may even be thinking about ways to begin planning some marketing activities for your business. You want to market something, and you want to take the right path.

You may have visions of what type of marketing you'd like to do—perhaps a website launch or a great advertising campaign; possibly you've considered an integrated email campaign. Maybe you're not sure what type of marketing activity you should do next and need some ideas. In any case, you're thinking hard about marketing. Well, good for you, but a word of advice—before you begin scratching out marketing activities and skipping ahead to the marketing template plan at the end of the book, I recommend that you stop a moment. Before you jump into any plan or invest in any marketing activity, read through the chapters and do the exercises in this book. Trust me, you'll be thanking me later.

Why listen to me? Well, I am a high-tech and consumer marketer with over 18 years of product and strategic marketing experience. I've worked with Fortune 500 companies, startups, and medium-sized, and non-profit companies doing a variety of marketing planning, launch development, and execution. I've worked with VPs of Marketing, and I've worked with CEOs, small-business owners, and product engineers. I've worked in companies that are on the verge of going public, and I've worked with companies that are just starting out from scratch that have no funding and no product! I've also worked with consultants, and I've been a consultant. In my experience, I've seen a lot of products and services marketed!

I wrote this book to help people make good marketing decisions. I want people to feel good about the marketing choices that they make for their businesses. I also wanted to introduce a fun and easy process that allows people to develop effective marketing plans! To get those effective marketing plans created, first and foremost, I know people have to take inventory of their overall business. People should take a step back to gather accurate information on where the business is going and what is happening in the business that is going right and wrong. I am convinced that the difference between a really effective marketing plan and a not so effective marketing plan is the relevant information available to each particular business. To make smart marketing decisions, I want people to have the necessary tools that will allow them to see what stage their business is in and what their customers are really thinking about their product or service.

Throughout my many years in marketing, I continue to see that business owners have difficulty looking at their business with an objective, open mind. This makes it very challenging to make smart decisions about marketing activities. I have witnessed very successful executives spend a lot of money on the wrong marketing activities that have no impact on their customers. I have also witnessed CEOs and VPs of Marketing as they waste away venture capital money on marketing activities that don't yield results and don't generate new customers. Tragically, when I think back to the 90s, especially during the high-technology boom, I see that a great deal of money was wasted on marketing programs that didn't work!

The Importance of Customers in Your Marketing Decisions

Unfortunately, business owners sometimes forget to consider their customers and potential customers when they make marketing decisions. It sounds crazy, but it's true! I can't tell you how many times I've seen a lack of consideration and awareness for how customers are viewing a product or service when it comes to planning marketing activities. Customers' needs evolve and change. Many business owners think they understand their customers, but they fail to see how their customers' needs may grow and shift. Events can happen every day to change a customer's mind. For example, the economy may impact a customer's decision about the way they typically buy a product or service. Or a management team switch may mean that your product or service may no longer be a priority for a business with new leaders at the helm. Even the addition of a new product or service or change in your own business strategy may no longer meet a customer's needs. Think about it—without fully understanding what your customers are thinking and wanting, you are challenged to plan meaningful marketing activities that effectively reach out to them.

Your customers seek and purchase your product or service, so their opinion should count first before you plan out your marketing strategies. Their perception of your product or service needs to be an ongoing part of your decisions as you plan out marketing activities. This means you really need to check in with your customers often and make it a point to see what's happening with how they are viewing your business. Your customers are most important to the success of your business and their perception of your product or service should be a critical component of your marketing decisions! You will learn how to assess what your customers are thinking about your product or services in this book and ask the right questions so that you are attuned with them.

EVALUATING YOUR BUSINESS: Why It's So Hard, Why It's So Important

There's a difference between working on your business and working in your business. Wouldn't you agree? When you're knee-deep in the day-to-day tasks of running your business or managing some part of your business, you are working within your business. You're busy! You don't have time to think about a lot of things besides driving the business. It's easy to get wrapped up in all the millions of tasks at hand like making payroll, managing your employees, selling your product or service, making sure your product works, and more. With all the many things that have to happen on a daily basis, it's hard to take a step back to see what's really happening from a big picture—a twenty thousand-foot level! Yet taking a pause to see what's really happening is so critical to the success of how you should market effectively to your customers.

To fully appreciate how to market your product or service, you really need to be able to look at your business objectively. What I mean by this is looking to see what is happening overall in your business. Look at all the successes, all the failures and what's truly happening with your customers. Sometimes marketing the obvious is not so obvious when you're working on the business! Marketing is also not an easy task when you are running your business and/or inside the business itself. When you can see what is really happening in your business, you have a greater chance of helping it to grow and can make the right marketing decisions moving forward.

In this book, the evaluation work you do will give you the opportunity to evaluate what's going on in your business. Once you understand this, you will have an easier time making marketing decisions that can move your company in a forward direction. Once you have done this analysis work, you may have a better idea of where it is exactly that you want to go with your company. Many companies struggle with where they want to go because the possibilities appear endless. Sometimes the most natural direction for the company doesn't seem logical. Or, many times, a company has trouble focusing in on core areas of the business that will generate the most revenue and give them the best opportunity to connect with their customers. In the coming chapter, you're going to get a great opportunity to pause from your day-to-day work tasks to analyze your business and build an effective marketing plan.

How You
Can Use This Book

This is a book for anyone who is looking for advice on how to market something. That something might be a product or it could be service. You may be a business owner, a CEO, or a marketing manager or executive. Regardless of who you are, and your knowledge of marketing, I promise that the steps you will be guided to take throughout this book will help in your marketing process and save you time and money before you invest in your marketing activities.

Throughout this book I use three business-owner examples to help you see how the interactive exercises can be beneficial for different types and sizes of businesses. These examples cover the following industries: automotive service repair, Human Resources (HR) consulting, and Information Technology (IT) services for small businesses. All of these business owners are at a particular stage in the growth of their business, and each one has a different type of customer. You may find that you identify with one business owner or all of them. One business is in startup mode, while another may have more established customers with a solid product. The way that these business owners approach their customers may vary, but they are all in need of marketing help in some form. Hopefully the business-owner examples used in this book will help you to understand that regardless of your business objectives and the type of product or service that you plan to market, there is great value in taking the time to do some analysis work before you dive into marketing activities.

You can use this book in segments or all at once. My recommendation is to read through each chapter and go through all of the exercises thinking about your own business as you do them. This will help to shed some light on where you are and unlock the code to some unique information that will best influence your customers. Some exercises may prove to be more useful than others, and you may decide that several exercises can be used successfully together while others may not work as well for you. In some cases, you may decide that you will continue to use an exercise repeatedly in the future planning stages of your business and its growth. This is great. All of the exercises can be useful in some way. Different sized businesses have different business needs and varied business models that help them grow and thrive. But all business owners need information to help them make good decisions. The process of gathering the information can be translated into any stage of your business, and the thinking behind these exercises will undoubtedly give you the framework you need to make better marketing decisions.

How This Book Is Organized

This book is a reference tool for you and your business. The content that you read along with the exercises that you complete will give you all the information you need to prepare a solid marketing plan for the next thirty, sixty, and ninety days. The work in this book has been designed to allow you to stop and take a look at your business objectively by listening to what your customers are saying and being aware of what your revenues are revealing and where your business is really going!

Designed for ease of use, this book is divided into three sections. Part I will give you an introduction (which you are now reading) along with an overview of marketing plans and when and why businesses use them. You'll also get a better understanding for how good solid business objectives can really help you develop your marketing activities.

In Part II, you will get a complete overview for how to evaluate your business through interactive and thought-provoking exercises. You will have examples to demonstrate how other companies have completed them, and then you will do the exercises on your own business. In your evaluation of your own business, you'll gather valuable information about your customers and your business. This information you gather will help you later when you get to the marketing plan template at the end of the book.

Finally, in Part III you will use a marketing demand tool to determine where you are in your business with regard to the demand for your product or service. This will be your guide to plan out some marketing activities that make sense for your business. After reviewing this tool and understanding where your product or service ranks in terms of demand, you will have access to some best practices and suggested marketing activities that make sense to pursue. It is then up to you if you choose to include these suggestions in your marketing plans. In Part III you will also find a simple marketing template—a handy tool to help you develop an ideal marketing plan customized for you and your business. Based on the information you've gathered from your interactive exercises, completing the template will be a snap to finish and will set you on a new course for your marketing activities.

You will find that marketing terms appear frequently in this book. The good news is that these marketing terms have been outlined and explained for you! You will see the definitions appear at the beginning of each chapter so you can refresh yourself on the term before reading the content in the chapters. So if you don't know what they mean when you first read the chapter, you will learn through reading the definition. In some cases, you may recognize these terms and in other cases, they may be new to you. The definitions provided in this book are here to help you understand how I am defining them with respect to the marketing self-evaluation exercises.

The interactive self-evaluation exercises are found in Part II. The interactive self-evaluation exercises are integrated into the chapter text and an exercise may pop up for you to complete as you are reading. These self-evaluation exercises are designed with you in mind and can be easily noted, so keep a pen/pencil handy for recording your answers. Yes—write in this book and keep it handy! This will allow you to think through your answers as you read through the chapters. At the end of each interactive exercise is a "Reflection" statement and "Reflection Exercise." These are designed to provoke you about the work you just did in the exercise and can help prompt new ideas and solutions as you continue reading about the planning of marketing activities for your business.

You may find yourself evaluating your business in a different light than you would on a typical day with these exercises, and the great thing is that they can be used over and over again. They will force you to think outside your typical thought patterns. You will be using a process that will help you to make better decisions about your marketing activities and those decisions will ultimately help you better market to your customer and drive your revenues. For example, you will be looking at what is working best in your business and how your customers currently view your business thus giving you a better understanding for what they value in your product or service. Your knowledge of their perception of what you are marketing to them will become critical in your. marketing plans. This information will change over time, so you can always go back and re-define your answers as your business evolves.

As you read this book, you may become aware that you're not sure exactly where you want your company to go, and that's okay. If you don't, it's at least good to have a strong understanding of where you think you'd like it to go in the next six months to a year, and the self-analysis exercises will help you to accomplish this. Use the exercises as a guide to help you determine where you might be headed. Once you get to the template at the end of the book, you may be surprised by how much you've learned by reading through these chapters.

Remember, you are in the driver's seat. Most of the information you will be gathering in the exercise work will give you some strong hints on the direction you need to go, but ultimately you are the decision maker in these plans. Once you set your marketing course, make no mistake: You're on the path to executing those plans. Taking your business self-evaluation seriously will help you to complete the exercises that will benefit your marketing activities for the long-term.

I hope you enjoy the processes in this book. My goal is to pass along the tools needed and necessary for you to complete a self-evaluation of your business. When it is time for you to develop your marketing plan, the process will be easy, fun, and interactive. Once you finish this book, I hope you can feel comfortable sharing what you've learned with co-workers, friends, and anyone else you believe would really benefit from knowing how to market something in a more effective manner.

Let's get started!

Chapter 3

Business Plans and Marketing Plans: Why and When Do Companies Use Them?

Imagine for a moment that you are building your dream house from scratch. Exciting, right? Along with your excitement and enthusiasm, there's no doubt it would take a lot of effort from many people to complete your ideal home. Many steps would need to be taken first. First, you would pick a property on which to build, and then you would purchase that land. Next, you'd work with an architect to create a detailed blueprint of your house. Finally, a contractor would take the blueprint and evaluate what would be needed before building. Many details and decisions would have to be made before your house was actually completed!

Think about the importance of your house blueprint. The blueprint is critical to building a house as it benefits many people: the city planning committee, contractors, builders, architects, the owner of the house, and the list goes on. Without a blueprint, your contractors wouldn't know how to begin building on your land, and they wouldn't know what materials to order. A blueprint is an essential tool for building your dream home, right?

Now consider your business. Similar to a house blueprint, your overall business plan impacts a number of people. Building a house is not the same as building a business; however, you couldn't build a house without a blueprint, and ideally, you wouldn't make important decisions about your business without first having some kind of plan. When I say plan, it could even be a verbally agreed upon plan with your key business stakeholders. Since your marketing activities should be aligned with your overarching goals for your business, it makes a lot of sense to evaluate your marketing activities on a regular basis. This evaluation process ensures that your marketing efforts help you achieve what you want for your business. Makes a lot of sense, right? Do you currently have a marketing plan? If so, take a moment to think about this: Does that marketing plan align with your current business objectives? Well, ideally, it should.

When to Use Business and Marketing Plans

So when should you use business plans, and when should you use marketing plans? It might help to review the difference between what a business plan does and what a marketing plan does. First, let's talk about a business plan. Typically a business plan is a blueprint for investors and the management team to provide a framework for how the company will grow and how revenues will be generated. Business plans are generally completed even before the company is launched—and often before it even receives funding—and then the plan gets strategic buy off from a number of individuals. Marketing plans are typically included in the business plan and provide a detailed overview of what will be marketed, how, and to what audience. Once this business plan is completed, not surprisingly, it may collect dust on a shelf. Once it's done it rarely gets revised again.

Marketing plans outline the marketing strategy for the company's product or service. However, marketing plans are living documents. They get referenced all the time, and they grow and change as the business grows and changes. Typically a marketing plan will include details like target audience, promotion and advertising strategy, and any messaging and product pricing plans as well. Tactics like the specific types of marketing activities, such as an email or direct mail campaign, are also included. A budget will often appear in the marketing plan to determine what will be spent over the fiscal year to cover the marketing strategy and tactics outlined in the plan.

So like a house needs a blueprint before it is built, a business needs both a business plan and a marketing plan to determine a strategy and a direction. This helps set the foundation for what the company plans to accomplish and gives some objectives for what types of marketing goals will help to meet those company goals. You may be wondering how often you should refer to a marketing plan. It really varies by organization and by individual. Some marketing people adhere to strict annual marketing plans and seldom deviate from those plans. In a large organization, planning with a budget ahead of time can be critical to a company's growth and measurement process. In a smaller organization, such as a startup, a marketing plan may evolve quickly, and its existence may depend on how many rounds of VC (Venture Capital) funding are available. Venture Capital is typically defined as an independently managed pool of capital best suited for rapidly growing or start-up organizations with a business plan. On average, a capital investment requires that twenty-five to fifty-five percent of the capital go to an investor. People use marketing plans in different ways, but a business plan is the starting point for any company's growth. Documenting a business plan helps the company's leadership team understand in what direction they are going and keeps everyone moving toward the same goals.

In general, marketing plans are typically done only once a year. However, if your company is growing and changing, it makes more sense to do a quick analysis of your marketing efforts every quarter instead of every year. This way you have a good understanding of what your business measurements look like, and you can make adjustments to activities that may not be working for your business.

Do you have a business plan? You may benefit from having that plan accessible while reading this book. You may also want to pull out the marketing portion of that plan and see what has already been documented. As you go through the exercises in the book, compare what you are learning to what you have already planned. If you don't have a current business plan available, don't worry. You can make a best guesstimate on the questions found in the exercises, and you will still be able to gather some very relevant material.

How Change Impacts Your Marketing Plan

So let's talk about change for a minute. Everyone knows that changes in business happen on a regular basis, and those changes can impact your business and your customers. Think back to the house blueprint analogy. If your architect made any changes to the blueprint for your dream house, imagine how many people would need to be included in this decision— everyone involved in your house project! Changing the dimensions of a room in your house could suddenly impact a number of very important planning decisions. Similarly, if you change direction in your business plan your marketing plan would also need to both follow suit and realign to match your new objectives, right? Of course!

Imagine that you or your CEO suddenly decided that you needed to change the type of customers you were going to go after. Maybe you decided to go after a completely different target market. This would impact your marketing efforts. Maybe this decision would send your company scrambling! It would certainly affect your marketing efforts and possibly your marketing budget. Many things would need to change. The messages you sent out to your customers would need to be repositioned. Your outgoing sales and marketing collateral pieces would need to be updated. Any presentations, website, and additional media would also need to be updated. The type of customers that you would want to talk to would be different, so you'd need to understand them better. There'd be a lot of work to do!

To market to your new audience, you would want to understand the best way to reach them and the best way to influence them. This could all be achieved through a new marketing strategy, but you would want to be certain that you'd thought about it first. A new marketing plan of action would really help you do this. Your previous marketing plan was driven by a number of already existing business factors. If you or your CEO wants to change the direction of the company, you also want to change your marketing activities to match your company's evolving needs. This allows you to maintain a competitive advantage when you are ready to market your product or service. But, how quickly could you come up with a new marketing plan, and how would you go about picking the right marketing activities for a new type of customer? If you have the right tools that allow you to evolve your plan, you can make smart marketing choices and can very quickly come up with a targeted marketing plan that will quickly grow your business.

The intention of your work in this book is to provide you with these tools. You will set the right marketing activities in motion to complement your business objectives as they evolve and change. To keep up to speed with how your company is evolving and changing, this book will help you develop an analysis of your company that can help you on an ongoing basis so that each ninety days you have a great reference tool ready to go. You'll look at your company, do some analysis work, and look at the marketing efforts you have done to date. With this information, it will be easier to plan effective marketing activities that make sense for you and your business as you are growing and changing.

The Importance of an Effective Marketing Plan

Some people find that writing and developing a marketing plan is quite easy, but executing that plan is a challenge. Why? Because it's hard to look at your company objectively and then make a plan and a budget that makes sense for your business and then stick to that plan. That's because it is difficult to look at your business with an objective mind—a fresh pair of eyes when you're in the business itself. When you are in the business itself, it's not as easy to see what is happening, what's working well, and what's not working, without being somewhat subjective. Also, if your company is growing and moving fast, there are a lot of things happening at once, so executing to plan may be even more of a challenge.

You may be thinking to yourself, "Well, if I'm going to be evolving my business constantly and my marketing plans needs to align with that plan, why bother doing a marketing plan since it may change? Does it really make sense to have one?" The answer is yes, and the truth is, an effective marketing plan can really help your business in a number of ways like grow your revenues and increase customer satisfaction. But you don't have to knock yourself out doing the plan.

Think a moment about what is making your business thrive today. No doubt it's a combination of factors that are making it run well. Your business is also going to have different phases. It may be growing fast one year and then just maintaining another year. You may have a year where revenues are declining. Whatever is happening, the business will be evolving as you gain new customers or lose customers. The point is, if your business is constantly evolving, the way you create and develop your marketing plan should evolve as well. And that means the marketing activities that you choose today may not be the same ones you choose in six months to a year.

So how can a marketing plan help you and your business? By creating an effective marketing plan and executing to that plan, you can move forward in the success of your business. Remember that you as a business owner, CEO, or manager will need to execute to the plan you build, and if you can, here's a summary of the ways that a good marketing plan can actually help you and your business:

- Set goals and objectives: Allows you, the business owner, a foundation for what you would like to accomplish in terms of sales and marketing objectives, allowing you to set milestones to accomplish.

- Measure: Gives you a starting point to measure the effectiveness of how you market to your customers and to measure how well your plans are working.

- Budget: Allows you to plan how you will market and what you can actually afford to spend on marketing.

- Commit: Powerful means to get you to commit to your ideas and to commit to the growth of your company.

- Analyze: Prompts you to analyze your message in terms of your customers. The way you reach out to your customers may have to change and evolve as your product or services change.

- Understand your customers even better: As you plan and evaluate your marketing activities, you will continue to gain a greater understanding of how your customers perceive your product or service.

- Change: As your business evolves and changes, your decisions to market differently to customers may be necessary. A good marketing plan will allow you to make updates as you take new direction for your business.

- Drive revenues: Ultimately, your marketing activities should help you drive customers and drive revenues. Understanding your revenues will help you to get a handle on what steps to take from a marketing perspective to continue increasing revenues in the direction you need.

An effective marketing plan is really a tool to drive you to your next destination in your business. However, if it sits on your shelf collecting dust with your business plan, it's going to do you no good! Sometimes companies do their marketing plans and fail to use them once they are developed. That's why in this book, you will be developing a useful plan that is customized to you and your business right now.

Your marketing plan will be evolving as fast as your business is evolving. At the end of this book, you'll have created a tool to help you in the next ninety days, and when those ninety days are over, you can go back again and re-evaluate your business, look at your progress, and re-use the template all over again. Then, with the information you have gathered from the self-evaluation exercises, you'll be able to re-create plans for the next ninety days, and the next, and the next, etc.

Identifying Your Strengths—Charting a Path for Successful Marketing Activities

In completing the book exercises, you will learn how to bring out the best qualities of your company, and be able to best articulate what you have to market and sell to your customers. Once you have identified those best qualities, you will be able to talk to your customers more clearly in your marketing efforts. In the process of doing your self-analysis work, you will gain valuable insight into how your customers think and feel about your product and how you are marketing to them. This is good stuff, right? You may also discover that your current marketing efforts may not be as effective as they should be, and in this process you will find new ways of attracting different types of customers. Additionally, the information you gain from reading and doing exercises in this book will give you some data to help you reach your short and long-term marketing goals.

Completing these exercises will also enable you to chart a path for successful marketing activities. This will include making some strategic and tactical decisions for what you need to be doing in the next thirty, sixty, and ninety days in your marketing efforts. What do I mean when I say strategic and tactical decisions? Making strategic decisions means a plan of action for your marketing activities. Making tactical decisions means creating the specific details or parts of your strategy that can be implemented to complete your plan—for example, creating a direct mail campaign, e-blast, or marketing promotion program.

PART II

The Twelve Self-Evaluation Marketing Exercises

IN THIS PART OF THE BOOK, you will be introduced to the twelve self-evaluation marketing exercises. These are interactive and thought-provoking exercises designed to provide important information about your business for your marketing plan. You will have the opportunity to read how other business owners did the exercises and what they learned. Then you can do the exercises using your own business as an example. In the reflection sections at the end of each chapter, you will find some additional questions that will help you to use what you've learned in your work to enhance your marketing strategies.

**Chapter
4**

What is the Purpose
of These Exercises?

et's discuss the marketing exercises in this book because they are very important. Your business is evolving and moving through changes on a quarterly if not monthly basis, right? As you plan your marketing efforts, you will need to keep up to speed with what is happening currently in your business. The questions in the exercises help to get you thinking so that you can provide yourself a dynamic framework for building a strong marketing plan.

The Twelve Self-Evaluation Marketing Exercises

There are twelve self-evaluation exercises in this book. Some of them are long and some of them are short, but if you complete all of them, you will be gaining a tremendous amount of information for your business.

Make sure you do the self-evaluation exercises using your business as your own example. Be diligent about finishing them, if you can. They will help you to set a course for your marketing activities. Once you do the self-evaluation exercises, I promise you will uncover some valuable information that will help you to get on track to a strong marketing plan of action. Here's a summary of the exercises and what you will learn:

- Exercise 1: Identify the value of your product or service.
- Exercise 2: Identify your core business offering.
- Exercise 3: Understand your product or service value from your customer's perspective.
- Exercise 4: Identify your business solutions to your target audience.
- Exercise 5: Define and understand your target audience.
- Exercise 6: Segment your customers.
- Exercise 7: Determine which segment you would like to grow.
- Exercise 8: Evaluate current trends that can advance your product or service.
- Exercise 9: Analyze your competitor's messaging and what's working well for them.
- Exercise 10: Analyze your revenues and how that may affect your marketing.
- Exercise 11: Understand what your business is doing right today.
- Exercise 12: Use the marketing demand tool to discover where your product or service fits in relationship to demand from your customers.

Once all exercises are completed, you will then use a marketing plan template in chapter 17 to plan out your marketing activities for the next ninety days.

I hope you are excited, because if you've followed my suggestions, you're well on your way to a great marketing plan for your business! I invite you to sit back, relax and get settled in. Enjoy the show of evaluating your own business. There is a lot of exciting and groundbreaking information that you will discover by doing these exercises in the book. The information you learn from completing the exercises will show you what type of marketing activities can work best for you and your business. Try to have fun with this, and let's go!

Identifying the Value of Your Product or Service

What does your product or service do, how does it work, and
how does it add value to your customer? In simple terms,
"Ahem…just what exactly are you marketing?"

imagine that you are at a party explaining your business to someone who has never heard of your business before. Think about what they might ask you. You would probably be asked about what your product or service did and the size of your business. There might even be some questions about how your product or service serves your customers. Since the person at the party is new to hearing about your business, whatever you presented about your business would impact their belief on what your product or service does.

I was at a party recently and I met a professional who wanted to talk about his business with me. I asked about his business and what his product did and he said "software." Great, I thought, "Tell me more." After fifteen minutes, he explained that he'd been marketing in China and the U.S., that he had a supply-chain product, that he had all kinds of potential customers and partners, and that it was going to change the way people did business. Then after fifteen minutes, I said, "Excuse me, but can you explain what exactly your supply-chain product does, how does it work, and how does it benefit your customers?" I love referring people to other businesses, so I wanted to be sure I really understood what his product did so I could find him some potential customers if I came across them through my network. In my experience, sometimes word-of-mouth marketing is the best way to gain new customers. He seemed to understand his business very well and talked a lot about his distribution strategies, but he couldn't seem to articulate into words how his product benefited his customer or how the product worked. I walked away from the conversation sort of scratching my head.

At the same party I met another business professional. She and I talked about our business backgrounds and she asked what I did, and I asked her about her business. In less than twenty-five words, she explained that she was a sales consultant. She clearly described that her business helped executives to bring in more sales revenues through her training programs. She and her team would provide coaching and strategy sessions with sales executives and their teams, helping them to set goals and objectives on a quarterly basis to grow their business. In a nutshell, she said her training programs were adding value to sales teams by making them more effective sales managers and that her programs were contributing to significant revenue increases for the companies she worked with. I walked away from that conversation with a very clear understanding of what she was selling to her customers and the benefit she was bringing to her customers with her sales training programs.

The point of these two stories is that people want to know what your company does, and they want to know what you are marketing! In many cases, people want to help you get your message out to your customers. Help them to understand by clearly identifying what your product or service does. It should take you no less than three minutes to summarize it, and if you can't summarize it in less than three minutes, learn how to! Make it easy for people to understand by clearly identifying what you do and how you benefit the customer in your business. It's that simple.

Adding Value to Your Customer's Life

There are some very valuable products and services out there that businesses are marketing! However, many companies forget to recognize the importance of how their product or service really adds significant value to the lives of their customers. When I say value add or adding value, what do I really mean? Adding value is increasing the worth of your business offering or product through a process. That process could be through your customer's perception, image, quality, performance, or even branding. It could be an increase in components to make your product or service run better such as a new product enhancement of a computer software program that makes it run faster or a new flavor for an ice cream product that tastes even better than before. The result of the process of input will help to increase the value of the output—the result is that the product becomes more valuable, more significant to your customers.

Understanding why your customers care about your product or service is essential to your marketing plan. The activities you select to market your business will depend on how your customer perceives your business and how their needs can be met by your solution. For example, you may discover that your customers are beginning to use your product in a different way. Some cell phone companies are recognizing that consumers are now looking for an all-in-one solution with their phone. Customers want to be able to check email, get to the Internet, and download photos all onto their phone! Phones are not just for talking anymore. Luckily, many phone companies are trying to come up with a variety of solutions on one handheld phone product. The iPhone is a perfect example of a company that is adapting to the needs of their consumers. Blackberry is another example. Their product allows email and phone capabilities on one product making it extremely convenient for business professionals.

As your customer's needs begin to shift and evolve, you'll need to understand why they are changing and incorporate those changing needs into how you are messaging your product or service. That's right; you will need to be flexible! Think back to your business and your product or service. How do you think you are adding value to your customer's lives?

EXERCISE 1: Identifying the Value of Your Product or Service

This exercise will help you understand how your product or service benefits your customers.

An Example: Mobile Mercedes Mechanic

Mobile Mercedes Mechanic is a self-owned mobile mechanic service located in Northern California. Jon, the owner, has been fixing, repairing, inspecting, testing, and working with Mercedes-Benz vehicles for over twenty-five years and has expertise working at both the factory and dealer level. As a trusted and reliable Mercedes-Benz mechanic, he frequently receives referrals from clients and business people who have worked with him and know that he has a great reputation for being friendly, professional, and knowledgeable. Jon trained in Germany for six years doing an apprenticeship. He earned his Meister degree in automobile repair in Northern Germany, giving him the legal right to teach his skills to others. His practical mechanic experience was acquired from working at the Mercedes-Benz factory located in Germany.

Unique to most mechanic service businesses, Jon's Mercedes service offers his customers a free diagnostic inspection of their Mercedes-Benz autos explained either in person or via phone. In many cases, inspection of their Mercedes-Benz autos gives Jon an opportunity to diagnose what problem exists, and he can quickly give an assessment of what needs to be done, how long it may take, and what the anticipated cost is. Jon did the following self-evaluation exercise on his business. Read how he answered this exercise, and then review new things he learned.

Mobile Mercedes Mechanic's Answers to Exercise 1

How do you discuss your product or service to customers? Describe in less than seventy-five words what your service does and how it benefits or adds value to the life of your customer.

Mobile Mercedes Mechanic is a privately owned car service business with twenty-five years of Mercedes-Benz expertise. Open seven days a week, it ise a completely mobile business, allowing customers the convenience of having someone come directly to their house or a location of their choice to take a look at their vehicle. The owner Jon, has twenty years of dealership and German factory experience, and he gives customers a free inspection diagnostic of their automobile.

Key Findings

What this self-evaluation exercise above reveals from reading the description above is that Jon's Mobile Mercedes Mechanic is an expert organization and he has a commitment to making the car service experience a pleasant and most convenient one for his customers. Understanding that he has over twenty years of dealership and Germany factory Mercedes-Benz experience establishes credibility and trust with customers almost immediately. For Mercedes-Benz owners, having someone understand their vehicle is of the utmost importance.

What do customers value in their experience with Mobile Mercedes? The value to the customer is that they can feel comfortable knowing that they don't have to bring their cars into a shop, because the service will come to them! It's a seven-day-a-week availability service. In addition, a free inspection diagnostic is given upon arrival allowing the customer to get a quick overview of what is wrong with the car immediately. The diagnostic of the car can typically be figured out in ten to fifteen minutes, which is extremely convenient and easy for the customer, saving time and money. In some cases, the diagnostic can be figured out over the phone. In a traditional dealership experience, a customer would leave their car and expect to wait up to a day for diagnosis. Mobile Mercedes customers value the fact that they can get an immediate diagnostic experience and can appreciate the years of experience behind the advice they are given!

Although this is not reflected in his answers in the exercise above, Jon realized after doing this exercise that his customers truly value the educational advice he gives when servicing their vehicle. Jon personally informs his customers about their vehicle, thus giving them an understanding of their car's service needs. He takes the time to share his Mercedes-Benz knowledge and training with customers, and he gets extremely positive feedback when he teaches them. Things that he discusses with his clients include anticipating long-term costs for their car, what it takes to keep their car running well, and expected budgeting costs for any future maintenance issues. He believes that his ability to share his knowledge and expertise is one of the primary reasons his customers continue to return. They love getting the personalized advice! Clients really appreciate this consultative quality to the business and know they are saving time and money with Jon's advice. They also enjoy learning new things about their Mercedes-Benz.

YOUR TURN: Exercise 1

Now it's your turn to do the exercise. Use the Mobile Mercedes Mechanic example above for reference if you need to.

How do you talk about your product or service to customers? Describe in less than seventy-five words what your product or service does and how it benefits or adds value to your customer's life.

Reflection

If you look back to the example with Jon at Mobile Mercedes Mechanic, it is evident that some of the things that are most valuable to his Mercedes-Benz customers may not be apparent in his current business marketing efforts. In looking at the owner's existing marketing materials, the educational benefits of the business service are not promoted, yet this is such an incredible asset to his customer base. Sharing this knowledge is not only valuable to his customers, but it is very much appreciated and sets him apart from other similar businesses. Since the owner is a natural at teaching people and he speaks German, he has the unique ability to translate even the most complex vehicle problems into a language that his customers can comprehend. Issues like budgeting, anticipating maintenance, and understanding how to keep a car healthy and in good shape for future tune ups seems to be of great importance to customers, yet these messages don't appear in any of the Mobile Mercedes marketing materials for potential customers to read. This truly would add value to his customers' lives and would serve to establish a solid and trusting long-term working relationship with new and existing customers.

Obviously, customers value the convenience of any business that is available seven days a week. They can also appreciate a personalized service and a diagnostic consultation that saves them both time and money. Jon has a unique opportunity to gain even more customers for his business through marketing the educational aspect of his business. Providing this type of specialized service will allow his customers to be informed, understand their cars, and receive value with each visit from their mechanic.

! — Reflection Exercise

Think back to your self-evaluation exercise above. Was it easy to articulate what your product or service does and how it adds value to your customer's life? What is unique that you do for your customers that may not be mentioned in your current marketing efforts? Are there any additional ways you add value to their lives that you do not mention? Is there anything in your expertise or your historical background that would be important for your customers to know about when they make a decision to use your product or service?

Get to the Core! Your Core Business Offering

What is a core business offering?
Your core business offering is any type of service or product
that essentially defines what you do best for your customer
and brings in the most revenue for your company.

hat do you do best for your customers? What is your core business offering? Many business owners are in such fast growth mode or so busy with other parts of their business that they forget to realize what they are doing best for their customers. Often times what they are doing best is the easiest thing to sell and market because customers already like the product or service. It should be fairly easy to market something that comes easily, right?

Identifying what your product or service does best is going to play an important part in your overall marketing plan, since you will be able to leverage what you do well to get to some of your long-term objectives. Have you heard the expression "Stick to your knitting"? Well, that's what I'm really talking about here. Your core business is what you do best for your customers, whether that is having a great quality product or providing a great quality service. Sticking to your knitting means really emphasizing your core business offering to customers and working in the area of the business that you know best.

In order to demonstrate how to do the following exercise, I'm using Mobile Mercedes Mechanic business as an example. Their core business offering is a convenient mobile mechanic service to customers who own Mercedes-Benz vehicles. The business offers customers a personalized service with the benefit of years of expertise. Owner Jon's experience with Mercedes-Benz vehicles allows him to be credible with customers as he is very good at what he does. Take a look at how the owner at Mobile Mercedes Mechanic answered this next self-evaluation exercise on his core business.

EXERCISE 2: Your Core Business and Value Add in Real-Time

This exercise will help you explore the key components of your product or service and identify how they help your customers.

An Example: Mobile Mercedes Mechanic

This example will also focus on Mobile Mercedes Mechanic, the company we introduced in the last chapter.

Mobile Mercedes Mechanic's Answers to Exercise 2

My core business is...

fixing Mercedes-Benz cars from a mechanic who offers a personalized experience for all customers. Customers receive a complete package of good service and years of Mercedes-Benz expertise along with a personality!

My product or service adds value to my customer by providing...

years of Mercedes-Benz experience with a personal touch. In addition, customers are charged by the job, not by the hour, providing a more affordable alternative to doing business with a Mercedes-Benz dealership. Customers also receive the added value of an onsite or phone diagnostic consultation.

...that helps them to...

feel comfortable and be well informed about the service detail they are getting for their vehicle.

As a result, they...

have a more personalized experience in a location of their choice. Through the owner's teaching process, the customers also become more educated on their vehicles, giving them a better understanding of what they are really buying with the service. This process gives customers an overall more positive experience with their car service

...than they would if they did not buy my service.

My service is offering...

a more personalized and educational approach to Mercedes Benz repair

...better than my competitors and/or other products or services.

YOUR TURN: Exercise 2

Let's identify the core business offering(s) for you and your business from your perspective. Think about what is at the core of your product or service and how it adds value to your customers. In a future exercise, we will look at your core business through your customer's perspective. For now, this exercise will help you to define your core business offering and determine your value to customers. Fill in the worksheet below with your business in mind. Use the Mobile Mercedes Mechanic exercise above if you need an example.

My core business is...

My product or service adds value to my customer by providing...

...that helps them to...

As a result, they...

...than they would if they did not buy my service.
My service is offering...

...better than my competitors and/or other products or services.

Reflection

Look back to see how the owner at Mobile Mercedes Mechanic answered the core business exercise. Clearly, his core business is offering a mobile mechanic service to Mercedes-Benz owners. But it's more than just a convenient service when you read through the exercise answers. What makes him unique is that he has a very personalized approach to his service through teaching clients about what is wrong with their cars, educating them through the entire process before it is repaired. As a result, customers feel more comfortable about their cars and come to trust the service they receive. The diagnostic approach also gives customers a chance to discuss their cars' problem before any work is begun, something that most dealers can't offer their customers. The overall business offering makes the car repair incident a much more comfortable experience overall for customers.

! ———————————————— Reflection Exercise

Think about the exercise you did using your company. What is it that you do best for your customers? What do you provide for your customers that makes their lives easier once they buy your product or service? Specifically, what makes your product or service unique?

Chapter 7

The Customer Lens

What is the customer lens? The customer lens is looking through the eyes of the customer. In clear terms, we will define the customer lens as essentially your customers' perspective in terms of how they think, feel and act with respect to your product or service—how your customers "see" you.

O kay, so now you have a good idea of what you *think* your product is, but do you know how your customers are viewing your product or service? Let's look through your customers' eyes for a moment. How would customers describe what your product or service does and how it helps them? If your clients were to recommend your product or service, what would they say is your core business? If you don't know the answer to this question, you may want to use the exercise below and take the time later to try an experiment on a current customer with whom you are close. Doing this next exercise, you may find that your customer may perceive value in your product through an entirely different perspective than yours—one you haven't thought of!

In general, most business owners do have an understanding (or think that they do) about what their customers value in their product or service. A growing business may still struggle with this, since they may have several offerings or products that are still waiting to mature. But even business owners who really know their customers must check in often with their customers to make sure the perception of their product or service hasn't changed. In some cases, a business may have many different products and offerings with many different types of customers. It pays to hear what your customers are thinking about your product or service offerings. Think about how many surveys you are asked to complete from some of your favorite companies. Those businesses are looking to get your feedback to determine if you've changed your mind about your favorite products and why. They also want to know if you are still a loyal customer. This is the sign of a company that cares about their customers—communicating with your customers and asking their opinion is a great way to find out why they keep coming back to your business!

Understanding Your Value (Through the Customer Lens)

We examined your customers' perception of your product and how that can vary by customer; however your customers' belief about your value may not be obvious to you and your business. They can have a very different perspective on your core business and product or service. This is good, if you know what that perspective is! Think about how you are adding value to your customers' lives. The next exercise can help you be certain about what your product or service does to create value, as you look through your customers' lens.

In some cases, you might ask your customers these questions and get their perspective. A good conversation with your customers is worth your time and money. Their feedback not only may be valuable, but also extremely enlightening. If you don't know how they would answer this question, think of one or two customers. If you asked them, think about what they would say.

EXERCISE 3: The Customer Lens—Understanding What Your Customers Value

In this exercise, you will find out what your customers truly value in your product or service as you look through their "customer lens."

An Example: P & A Human Resources Consulting Company

P & A is a small Human Resources (HR) management consulting services firm offering a variety of HR consulting services to their clients. Their services include recruitment, "strategic staffing" (helping organizations understand what they really needed in key positions beyond the technical skills listed on job descriptions), organizational development, performance management and management coaching, as well as HR policy development and implementation. The firm also provides recruitment services for a fellowship program at a large government agency. P & A has been very successful with a number of financial services firms and non-profit organizations. The principal of the P & A continually offers excellent service at reasonable costs to her clients.

When we sat to evaluate and discuss her core business, I asked her what she thought were the main reasons why her clients were interested in her service. I showed her the exercises used in this book and asked her to answer them visualizing her customer and looking through her "customer's lens." Interestingly enough, she learned a lot from doing these exercises. To answer the questions, she thought about how her customers would fill out these exercises and what they would write about her service. To answer these questions, she directly spoke with her clients.

P & A HR Consulting Company's Answers to Exercise 3

If your customers were to recommend your product or service, what are the most significant things that they would say about your core business?

1.) *Superior recruitment services (including knowledge of human resources and employment law) at a reasonable cost.*

2.) *Quick turnaround time/response time when client asks for a project or advice on a project.*

3.) *Integrity*

4.) *Judgment is also important to client.*

Next, P & A's principal asked her customers what they valued in her product or service and what they would say about the types of work that she offers to make their life easier/better.

The company where I buy/hire my...

HR consulting service product or service

...is...

P & A Management Consulting.

Their service adds value to my business by providing...

knowledgeable consultation on HR issues and a results-oriented recruitment process

…that help me to…

> *better manage our business and make good judgment decisions*
> *about our potential employees as well as our current employees.*

As a result, I can…

> *manage*

…more effectively than I did prior to engaging with this company. This company provides…

> *Recruitment and HR consulting with the added value of the*
> *principal's many years of experience which has allowed us to*
> *receive superior judgment and experience with all projects that she*
> *completes for us*

…with more value than do other companies in the marketplace.

Key Findings

In talking with her clients recently about what they valued in her; P & A's principal learned that that her judgment was actually at the top of their list! Their executives found that her unique background and experience had given her the type of judgment to recruit the right talent for their organization. At the same time, her judgment on a variety of human resources issues made her a reliable and trusted resource to the executive management team. They often called her to "run things by her" when they had tough decisions to make, and they wanted her "buy off" and support during these times. Although her years as an HR executive were important to the client, and her responsiveness to recruitment needs was appreciated, it was her judgment on which they relied for difficult issues that was the most valued service.

So using the P & A HR consulting company example, remember that your product or service may often have value in many different ways to your customers. The perception of what your business does may be different to different people. But you're going to have to ask the customer! Once you gather this information, you will find that it will be very helpful in your marketing efforts and plans.

Be certain that you know how your customers perceive your core business product or service so that you can determine how you want to address this in your marketing activities. Also consider that your customers may be viewing your product or service in a variety of ways. For example, your product may serve more than one purpose for your customers. As a product example, a new dental toothpaste product on the market cleans your teeth, whitens your teeth, and gives you fresh breath. This is all one product, but customers may perceive the core business of this product to be a teeth whitener even though the product was initially introduced as toothpaste. Remember, there could be many reasons why your customers come back time and again to purchase your product or service. Make sure you understand what those reasons are.

YOUR TURN: Exercise 3

Now, it's your turn to do the exercise. Consider asking your customers these questions in person, but if that is not possible, follow the exercise by imagining yourself in your customers' shoes.

If you asked your customers to recommend your product or service what are the three things that they would say about your core business? What do you provide that is most valuable to your customers? If your customers were to recommend your product or service, what are the most significant things that they would say about your core business?

You can do this for multiple customers if you want:

The company from whom I buy (where I shop for) my…

…is…

Their service adds value to me by providing…

…that helps me to…

As a result, I can…

…more effectively than I did before I found this company. This company does…

better than other companies out there in the marketplace.

Key Findings

If you weren't able to fully complete the exercise above, don't worry. Now that you have the template for the exercise, you can reach out to some customers and complete this information. Think about the best way to assess your customers. It may be an informal discussion in person or via phone. Most importantly, you want to get this information as accurately as possible. If your customers are loyal and want to help your product or service improve and continue to provide them with a solution, they will most likely engage in this exercise. This is also a good exercise to use repeatedly as you develop stronger relationships with your customers. If you feel uncomfortable asking these questions directly, create a survey. Surveys are great ways to find out specifically what your customers value. And once you have good relationships with your customers, no doubt you will be able to easily get this information since you may be in deep conversations with them anyway on an ongoing basis. Once you have this information, keep it handy. Use it on a quarterly basis to continue to understand your customers' perspective and to evaluate what makes customers keep coming back for more.

The point of this exercise is for you to realize what your customers are valuing in your product or service. As long as you can continue to understand the ways they are using your product or service, you can be steps ahead in your marketing planning. This exercise will prove useful when you determine which of your marketing activities will be your priorities for your customers.

You may be thinking, "Uh oh! Wait a minute here! How do I market successfully to my customers now that I know that they view my product differently than the way I'm currently marketing?" Don't panic. The purpose of these exercises is to make certain that you focus on your core business services, so you do not forget to address the variety of valued solutions and services that you provide from the same product or service. Remember my mention of the toothpaste product that not only cleans your teeth, but also acts as a whitener and a breath freshener? Obviously, this type of product is valuable from a variety of perspectives and customers may be buying for more than one reason! Simply put, make sure you remember the various customer lenses that may exist when looking at your product or service!

Get to know what your customers are thinking about when they look at your product or service and understand that their minds may change as their own needs change.

Looking through the customer lens is an educational and valuable exercise. Hopefully you have learned when looking through the customer lens, you see that there are more than a few ways your customers are viewing your product or service, and you can translate this into your marketing efforts. When we get to the marketing plan, we'll be drawing from this exercise above and address some of the attributes you've listed out.

Reflection

When P & A did the exercise, the principal of the firm learned that her judgment was incredibly valuable to her customers. She also learned that her clients valued the fact that their management team could best manage their business with her on board as a consultant. Although she's not currently using these messages in her communications to potential clients, she is considering this information. To address improving her marketing messages, she is considering using testimonials from clients who value her judgment and including this in her service brochure and collateral materials.

! ———————————————— Reflection Exercise

Looking through the customer's lens, did you uncover anything you didn't know before you started this exercise? Did you find that some of your customers had similar things to say about your product or service? Or possibly, some of your customers may have had different things to say about your product—things that you didn't even know added value. Hopefully you were able to discover some new and unique ways that you are adding value to your customers! What is working well with a particular customer and proves to be of value may also be of value to a potential customer. For example, if your customer is willing to share how your product solves a particular problem for their business, use that information as a quote in your marketing literature and your website to showcase how your product or service can benefit different types of customers.

Identifying Your Business Solutions to Your Customer

What is a business solution?
A business solution solves a problem for your customer;
it is a combination of products or services that enable resolution
to a particular problem or issue that a business faces.

ost businesses have problems or issues that need to be dealt with on a daily basis. These can be small or large issues. Some businesses have internal issues with employees or organizational process, while others have issues with their product or service. Regardless of what is needed, we rely on people and products to help enhance our lives to make it better.

Customers want to purchase products and services that make their lives easier. Business solutions help to sell a product. They want to know that what you are selling addresses specific problems or issues that they face. As we go into the next exercise, consider your product or service as providing a solution for your customers that helps them to do something faster, better, more efficiently, and helps them feel better.

Think about your business. Why are customers caring enough to purchase your product or service, and why do they choose you over another business? What are you offering that no one else is doing, and what makes you stand out from the competition? What critical issues or concerns are you currently addressing to help your customers, and what solutions do you provide? Let's take a look at some exercises that will help you identify your business solutions more closely.

EXERCISE 4: Identify Your Business Solutions to Your Target Audience

In this exercise, you will learn about the key issues or concerns that your customers could be facing and identify the business solutions that you can offer.

An Example: Mobile Mercedes Mechanic

Think back to the example of Mobile Mercedes Mechanic. While doing this book's exercises, Jon confessed that in many cases, most of his customers had encountered a negative experience receiving car service from a Mercedes-Benz dealer. With that being said, before they called Mobile Mercedes Mechanic for service and help, they were hoping to have a different kind of experience and a better experience with their car service. When the owner, Jon, did this next set of exercises, he was able to focus in on the critical issues and concerns that his customers faced before they took their car in for service at his company. In this next exercise you will start thinking about your customers' concerns and issues and what your product or service does to help remedy those concerns.

Mobile Mercedes Mechanic's Answers to Exercise 4

What are your customers' critical issues and concerns and what business solutions are you providing them to make their lives easier or better? List out the top three issues and concerns that your customers are facing and the business solutions you can offer your customers. Read below to see how Mobile Mercedes Mechanic answered the exercise.

Document the top three issues and concerns that your customers typically face and the business solutions that you provide with your product or service.

What is your customers' most critical issues and concerns?

Time and convenience: People don't typically have a day to take off work in order to drop off and pick up their car for service. If something happens to their car, it is very inconvenient to their lives to get the car fixed.

What is the business solution that you provide?

Mobile Mercedes Mechanic is mobile! Jon can go the customers' locations and can quickly provide a diagnostic consultation. This consult can also be done over the phone. This provides the customer with an immediate solution to their car problems.

What is your customers' second most critical issue or concern?

Trust and Expertise: Customers are looking for a mechanic with excellent experience and someone they can trust.

Customers love their Mercedes-Benz cars. They want someone to work with who is credible and who has expertise in this luxury car. Most customers are very afraid to leave their precious car with just "anyone"!

What is the business solution that you provide?

Business solution: The owner of Mobile Mercedes Mechanic, Jon, is most often the person who provides the diagnostic and fixes the cars. He has over twenty-five years of Mercedes-Benz experience and he knows these cars inside and out. He is credible, honest, and treats his customers' cars with respect. There is little that Jon does not know about the Mercedes-Benz car and he is accessible to his customers seven days a week.

What is the third most critical issue or concern for your customer?

Cost and shopping for a better deal: Customers are very cautious about how they spend their money on their car, and they are looking for a good deal on mechanic service. They don't want to be nickel and dimed for every single mechanical fix while their cars are in the shop. Reluctantly, many Mercedes-Benz owners go to a dealership for service because they think a dealer will know their cars best.

What is the business solution that you provide?

Business solution: Jon, of Mobile Mercedes Mechanic, will compare quotes with their customers and will explain what they are receiving for each quote. In addition, Jon is willing to work with customers on a cost and look for long-term solutions to fix the cars, wanting to add value to their experience. Mobile Mercedes Mechanic can provide Mercedes-Benz car owners a better experience than they would from the dealers and at a more reasonable cost. They also don't charge for every detail and fix needed on the car. For example, most dealers charge individually for everything that has been done to the car line item, by line item while in the shop. Mobile Mercedes Mechanic charges customers only by the project or overall job, again looking to provide a valuable service package to customers instead of an hourly charge.

Key Findings

Shown in the exercise above, Jon has addressed the critical issues and concerns of his customers: time and convenience, experience, trust, and cost. These are the main issues that come up before the customer even picks up the phone to ask for help from Mobile Mercedes Mechanic. Immediately, Mobile Mercedes Mechanic solves the problem of time and convenience. Since his business model is based on a mobile-service offering, Jon puts customers at ease with no need to drop their car at a dealer and go through the hassle of renting or borrowing a car for the day. From a convenience perspective, Mobile Mercedes Mechanic provides their customers with an easy and most convenient alternative to taking their cars to a dealer or shop.

In terms of customers needing experience and wanting trust, Jon's experience provides a great solution to this critical need. His factory and dealership experience allow him to provide a quick diagnostic consultation for his customers this being an incredible solution for those people who don't have a lot of time. His experience also lends immediate credibility in the eyes of the customer. In addition, instead of staying competitive with the dealers, the owner takes the time to walk through any existing estimates with the customer to explain what they are really getting and is willing to work out a plan for costs that work for the customer. Given the example above, Jon, of Mobile Mercedes Mechanic business, has addressed his customers' critical needs and concerns well.

Again, it is your turn to do the exercise. You are going to be asked to identify what critical issues and concerns your customers typically face and then give business solutions to resolve these critical problems.

YOUR TURN: Exercise 4

What are the three most critical issues and concerns that your customer faces?

1.)

2.)

3.)

Consider the business solutions that your product or service offers to resolve these critical problems and list them below.

Some business solutions that I offer my customers based on these critical issues and concerns include:

1.)

2.)

3.)

Reflection

Customers like to buy a service or product because it solves a problem, but often times there's more to it than that. Sometimes a number of problems come up before a customer makes a purchase and a combination of factors make them decide to go with a specific purchase. In the Mobile Mercedes Mechanic example, car repair is clearly solving a customer problem. But when the owner completed this exercise, three critical issues and concerns stuck out for his customers: time and convenience, cost, and the trust factor. All of these issues and concerns were considered critical for a majority of his customers, and these were what he could resolve with either his expertise or knowledge. The trust and experience was a critical problem that the owner listed as the second most important issue. The trust factor can be the main reason as to why a customer goes with a business or its competitor. Owners of a luxury car care and feel protective about who fixes their car. The Mercedes-Benz owner no doubt wants to feel that in addition to great and fast service, they are getting a good cost and that the mechanic is extremely knowledgeable.

Reflection Exercise

Review the critical problems for your customers and the business solutions you can provide. Do you talk to your customers about the business solutions you can offer them and discuss how you can solve their problems? Have you considered using the business solutions you outlined above in your marketing messages to customers? Clearly, they solve a critical business problem and make the lives of your customers much better! Your existing customers and potential customers need to know this!

Chapter
9

Identifying and Connecting With Your Target Audience

What is a target audience?

The term target audience is typically referred to as a community you have selected as being the most appropriate arena for your marketing or advertising campaign efforts. This community is composed of potential primary buyers or users of your product or service. They may be defined in demographic or psychographic terms. This is the group of people you want to reach out to and talk with in all your marketing and communication efforts!

et's examine your company's target audience. When I say target audience, I mean the group of potential customers you want to persuade and/or influence to buy or use your product or service. You may have several target audiences that you reach. Besides the industry itself, what does your target audience look like? Are they all males or females and do they fall into a certain category in terms of their job titles or expertise?

Profiling Your Customer

Who do you actively try to reach in your marketing efforts? It's important to get a picture of what your target audience looks like before marketing to them. I don't mean just physically, but it helps to know as much about them as possible. You can get this information through online marketing surveys, informal phone interviews, focus groups, market research studies, and digging into your own existing customer database information. I call this "profiling your target customer." Let's take a moment to profile your target customer. Part of a good marketing plan is having a solid understanding of what your customer is all about. What motivates them, what inspires them and what makes them tick? First, let's talk about your target customer by their role/function in their organization and their expertise.

What Does Your Target Audience Do?

Think about how your customers are divided in terms of their titles and roles. What types of responsibilities do they have day in and day out and what priorities govern their primary business decisions? Do you know what a typical day looks like for your target audience person? Understanding their priorities and what your company can do to help make their lives easier will be critical to your marketing messages. Using what you know about your customers can make your marketing messages even better. The more information you have, the easier it is to predict a customer's behavior. Once you establish what benefits your customer and what makes your customer tick, you can use this to your advantage by understanding what messages and/or pieces are most appropriate and can impact your customer.

Target Audience versus Decision Maker

Based on some of the marketing work you may have already done in your business, you may have determined that there is more than one customer audience you should be talking to, and that's okay. Some companies actually target one audience for their marketing messages but the decision maker (person who makes the buying decision) is another target audience that also needs to be influenced to buy. In some companies, salespeople actually target the decision maker to make a sale, while marketing may work on addressing a more general audience. Some companies have more than just a few target audiences per product or service. For example, if a company has several divisions with various different products, they may be targeting up to ten or fifteen different types of people with their product lines.

Make sure you know the difference between your decision maker and your target audience! You can learn this information by asking your customers or talking to your sales team. Learn this and distinguish carefully! In some cases, the target audience may also be the decision maker, but in many companies, this is not the case. A product or service might be needed in a department or group, but someone else makes the purchasing decision and will also need to be influenced. For example, if you have a technology product that helps make the life of the Information Technology (IT) manager easier, you will want to target this person. However, if the CIO is the decision maker, you will want to include this person in your marketing as well, because this person will decide whether or not your product will be accepted and if the invoice will be signed! Just keep in mind that both your target audience and the decision maker should be considered in your marketing messages.

What Does Your Target Customer Profile Look Like?

You should know your target customer like you know some of your dearest friends. This sounds a bit far-fetched, but really, you should know your customers well enough to understand what makes them tick. As I mentioned before, you can do some customer profiling through online marketing surveys, informal phone interviews, focus groups, market research studies, and digging into your own existing customer database information. You may already have quite a bit of information about your customers but don't have it documented. For example, if you have been selling your product or service to your customers for a long time, you may feel like you know your customers quite well and know their likes and dislikes like the back of your hand. You most likely won't know every detail about your customers, but see if you can answer some of the following questions about your customers:

- What types of publications do they tend to read?
- What companies do they find credible?
- What research reports would get them to take notice?
- What types of online newsletters and papers would impact their purchasing decisions?

- What favorite conferences that they would likely attend?

- What types of business associates may influence a decision and/or help them to give your product or service a better name?

- What influences their purchasing decision—is it price or performance? Or is it something else?

- What is their general age range, and what are their purchasing likes and dislikes (if available)?

- If they already buy your product or service, what keeps them coming back for more? What (if any) other products and services do they buy that may compete with yours?

- In their current day-to-day activities, what takes up the most time in their job and what are some of the challenges in their own role?

The answers to the questions above are important, because they can help you to identify the motivating factors that influence your customer's purchasing behavior, and the answers can help compile your "customer profile" for your own target audience. Once you have this "customer profile" it can be a useful tool for your marketing efforts. If you don't have many answers to the questions above, find a way to get them. These are questions that make up the profile of who you are marketing to, and knowing this information will help you greatly when you plan specific marketing tactics.

Let's discuss the questions above. When you read the questions, how many of the answers did you know? If you could identify answers to at least four or five of the bullets above, you have a general idea of who your customer is. But, it will definitely pay off to continue learning more about your customers. Once you have all this information, it's a great idea to keep it in a database as a "saved profile," and you can update it by keeping in touch with your customers through phone surveys, market research, or informal interviews. Make sure you keep updated on what your customers are doing and know what types of resources they are using to keep current on their new interests. As I mentioned, surveys are a great way to do this along with in-person meetings and discussions. If you can manage to release a quarterly if not bi-annual online or print survey to your customers to find out this information, you will be keeping current on your target customers, and your customers will be happier knowing that you have taken the time to understand what they like and dislike.

Talking to Your Target Audience

If you answered the questions above and you feel that you know your target audience, how do you talk to them in your marketing efforts? Do you use words and phrases that make sense to them so that they'll respond when you market to them? I can't emphasize this enough—the words that you choose to convey your key product or service offerings are extremely important to your target audience. If your target audience doesn't understand what you are marketing, then you are missing a great opportunity to sell your product or service. To be most effective in your marketing efforts, you need to learn how to talk to your customers in their own language!

You may have already established some marketing activities for your company that may include brochures, a Website, or direct mail and email campaigns. Or you may have just started your business, and the only thing you have right now to convey your messages is in a power point presentation format. Think about your existing marketing pieces and reflect on the content that they have. When you try to reach out and talk to your customers, what are you saying about your product or service, and what types of words have you been using to attract your target audience? Are you using words and marketing messages in current marketing activities to drive your target customers to your product or service? What phrases are you using to target your customers?

Below find examples of marketing pieces for attracting your target customer:

- Advertising Logo/tagline
- Newsletter with information on your company, product, or service
- Company overview or summary information in your brochures, collateral
- Power Point presentations for new customers
- Articles in trade publications that feature your product or service
- Boilerplate summary of your company on a datasheet, white paper, or press release

All of these examples can include messaging to your target audience and that's why the same message needs to stay consistent! You never know when a customer or potential customer will read about your company. If they continue to read the same messages, you increase the possibility your product or solution will be remembered.

Messaging to Your Target Audience: Make it Consistent

Lewis Carroll once wrote, "What I tell you three times is true." I think this is probably the case with messaging to your target audience, although it should hear what you have to say more than three times! Have you ever heard that a person needs to read and see an advertisement at least seven times before they remember what it said? This can be applied to your target audience; it needs to hear your message repeated over and over again. Marketers believe that repeated messaging helps to influence decision makers. When you determine your message, you need to repeat it and keep it consistent in all your marketing efforts whether it is direct mail, your website, or your newsletter. Keep your message consistent!

One day a potential customer who is in your target audience may see your Website, and the next month this customer may see your ad; it is important that your message is consistent and is easy to remember. You want to be remembered, not forgotten! Don't change your message midstream. Pay attention to what you are sending to your target audience. Be consistent and clear enough in your messages so that you are easily understood.

Exercise 5: Profiling Your Target Audience

In this exercise, you will get an idea about those who are in your target audience and learn what makes them tick.

An Example: NowMy Networks

NowMy Networks is a small organization of less than fifty employees that provides enterprise Information Technology (IT) solutions to small and medium businesses. Think of them as an "outsourced IT department." Their core business offering is working as a company's outsourced IT management group. They have a comprehensive, business-sensitive approach to supporting the information systems needs of fast-growing organizations. With their technology expertise, they give businesses a competitive advantage by allowing them to focus on their core competencies. By using cutting edge business processes and technologies, NowMy Networks also gives businesses an opportunity to increase their efficiencies and their revenues.

When both the founder and CEO (Raj Saxena and James Bland) at NowMy Networks discovered the exercises in this book, they were eager to try them out on their business since they was looking to revamp the company's marketing efforts in the following quarter. In terms of a target audience, the CEO thought he really understood who his main customer was and who he was targeting, but he really wanted to make some specific changes in how the company could better communicate to their target audience. Read below to see how Raj Saxena and James Bland answered these exercise questions.

NowMy Network's Answers to Exercise 5

What does your target audience look like?

The main target audience for NowMy Networks includes small-business owners who have a minimum of twenty employees and who are growing. Ideally, these small-business owners may have multiple office locations (between two and four).

Target Audience Details: What is the age and expertise of your target audience?

Our target audience is…

no specific age range

and their expertise area is…

generally biotechnology, semiconductor, and medical software

Our target audience is composed primarily of business owners.

When I break them out by percentage, here is what they look like:

NowMy Networks Customers—broken out by percentage

- *65% business owners*
- *30% CFOs, IT directors*
- *5% president, personal contacts*

Who is the target audience and who is the decision maker?

The target audience for NowMy Networks is …

a small business owner, CFO IT director or president

The key decision maker for NowMy Networks is…

a small-business owner

Key Findings

When NowMy Networks completed the percentage breakout of the types of customers they had, it was clear that a majority of their key business was coming from business owners. This was good news, since they were already deliberately targeting this group. Although CFOs and IT Directors were also included, they did not represent the largest number in NowMy Networks customer base. In addition the founder had listed personal contacts as making up a small percentage. These were people who had become customers through referral and were presidents of companies and in many cases the founder knew them personally.

NowMy Networks' main target audience is the small-business owner. The key decision maker is often the small-business owner because typically the owner is in charge of paying bills and is generally responsible for the success of the business. The Raj and James said they are aware that a small-business owner is both the influencer and the decision maker. Since NowMy Networks typically deals with smaller companies, Raj and James find it easy to identify both their influencer and the decision maker, while in a larger company this may not be the case.

EXERCISE 5: Customer's Key Drivers for Purchasing Your Product or service

In this exercise, you will learn about what motivates and drives your customers to actually purchase your product or service.

NowMy Network's Answers to Exercise 5

What motivates customers to purchase your product or service? What is their key driver?

The key driver for customers purchasing NowMy Network's IT service is their need for IT outsourcing and ability to increase their sales through the use of the technology that NowMy NetWorks teaches and provides.

Generally business owners want to save costs, and business owners are also looking for ongoing maintenance help that will ensure their peace of mind when it comes to their technologies. As a side note, customers have expressed that they keep coming back to NowMy Networks because the team has a skill for educating the small-business owner about the IT services that are truly needed for maintaining and growing an organization.

Looking at how NowMy Networks answered the exercise above, the key drivers for customers purchasing their services include:

- Immediate need for IT help, onsite support;
- Business owners needing to increase their sales for their businesses, education, and technology;
- Business owners needing a reliable resource to support IT services;
- Business owners needing to understand their business IT costs. NowMy Networks employees offer a simple education process about what is actually needed to maintain IT services that will support an organization.

Key Findings

After doing the exercises, I asked Raj and James if they were addressing these key drivers in their marketing efforts. They explained that their goal was for a new marketing launch for the following quarter.

From completing the previous exercises, Raj and James now understand that cost is a large issue for their customers. They also noted that while their customers are trying to cut costs, their small-business owners feel that IT guys are very expensive to hire. On average, NowMy Networks small-business owner customers are spending $3,000-5,000 monthly on IT costs and still feel like they are having IT problems! These customers were typically five to twenty-five employees-per-shop businesses, and were frustrated and confused by IT services. They appreciated having an educational review of what it really takes to run the IT side of their business. Since the employees at NowMy Networks are skilled at educating customers, the small business-owner customers they serve know that they are getting a bonus to their services. In addition to receiving IT help, they get ongoing educational assistance in learning about IT systems and products that help their business run more efficiently.

Developing a Specific Type of Solution to Help a Target Audience

As a solution to really help their target audience, Raj and James talked about plans for developing a new leasing-model structure. This leasing-model package will be targeted specifically to help small-business owners. This would be a service package allowing customers to lease out both IT help and support including hardware and software services and support, all covered in one bill. Since small-business owners are concerned about controlling cash flow, making this type of package available would be extremely valuable and convenient. NowMy Networks' marketing messaging for this package is planned to be included in their Website and all collateral materials for their next quarter.

EXERCISE 5: What Type of Messaging Are You Currently Using to Target Your Audience?

In this exercise, you will examine the key messages you are using to communicate with your target audience.

NowMy Network's Answers to Exercise 5

It was interesting to find that NowMy Networks is already addressing specific messages to attract their target audience—the small-business owner. When asked what messages they were using to address their target audience and key decision makers in current marketing materials (including Website, brochures, sales presentations, corporate pitches, and promotional messaging) this is their answer:

NowMy Networks believes that they need to add a personal touch in marketing to their target audience. Since their primary audience is the small-business owner, they know that doing business with them requires much personal connection and relationship work. How does NowMy Networks talk to their customers with their messaging? Their current messaging includes:

- *NowMy Networks shows photos of all IT employees on their website. The photos capture the IT workers and their personalities.*
- *NowMy Networks offers a money-back guarantee to all customers.*
- *Messaging includes wording that is easily understood by small-business owners who are focusing on running their business. Words such as "saving costs", testimonials from real customers, educating the customer, "how to increase the small-business owner's bottom line", and "itemizing the true costs of IT services" are really helping NowMy Networks to attract the customers they want to* serve.

Key Findings

By personalizing their services, Raj and James want their target audience to find that NowMy Networks is an easily approachable company and group of people. They also hope to make the IT process appear less intimidating, and they want to give current customers the assurance that they can return for more services. Friendly photos of IT employees are showcased on the NowMy Networks Website with the hope that customers visiting the Website will feel good about having a friendly-appearing face visiting their offices. This is a smart approach, since many small-business owners want to feel that they are doing business with other small-business people who are approachable and who can be trusted. Having this personalized approach, NowMy Networks hopes to attract small-business owners who want that "business-next-door approach" from another small-business owner.

For future messaging, NowMy Networks hopes to announce to the public that they have free audio and video informational materials and announcements on saving IT costs for small-business owners. They are currently working on a white paper to address the cost issues that small-business owners typically face. The leasing-package solution we discussed earlier in this chapter will also appear soon on their Website as a full-service offering to small businesses that truly will benefit from IT help.

YOUR TURN: Exercise 5

It's your turn now to do the target audience exercise! Consider your target audience to do the exercises below.

Profiling Your Target Audience

Target Audience Details: What is the age and expertise of your target audience?

(Describe them as best you can).

Their age range is….

And their area of expertise or areas of expertise are…

If you were to break up your customers by percentage, using 100 percent as a total, what would they look like?

%_____

%_____

%_____

Who is your target audience and who is your decision maker?

Your target audience is....

Key decision maker is....

Key drivers for customers to purchase your product or service

What is the key driver of customers for purchasing your service or product?

List out these key drivers for your target audience:

Are you currently focusing on any of these key drivers in your marketing messages?

Talking to your target audience: What types of messaging are you currently using to target your audience?

(Include messaging that you are using in your Website, collateral, advertisements, presentations, promotional materials, and email or direct mail letters.)

Reflection

When NowMy Networks completed these exercises, they were clear that their target audience was also their decision maker and that they intend to target the small-business owner. They now understand how to talk to their target audience and are proactive in focusing on the right messages in their existing marketing materials. They have also learned (through getting to know their target audience) that each of their customers requires a unique solution when addressing their cost and IT concerns. Once this was understood, they developed a product (the leasing package) specifically for their customers' needs and are working on ways to talk with customers about this new product. This new leasing package product gives small-business owners the opportunity to save on their IT costs, yet it also allows them the opportunity to have a single billing for their IT services, a huge convenience for small-business owners. Now, with this new program, small businesses can preserve their cash flow and at the same time receive ongoing IT maintenance to help their business thrive and grow. The creation of this program is an excellent example of how identifying your target audience will result in a marketing tactic that motivates your target audience to return for more of your services or products.

!
────────────────────────────── Reflection Exercise

Again consider your target audience and your decision maker. What types of key messages and tactics have you found that would be most appealing to your target audience and your key decision maker? Are there some similar messages that could apply to both? What types of special solutions or programs can you offer your target audience now that you understand this audience better? Are you addressing your target audience's key motivating drivers in all your marketing materials today? Think about ways that you can talk to your target audience in ways that truly speak to their likes and needs.

Chapter 10

Segmenting Your Customers

What is customer segmentation? To make it simple, customer segmentation is defined as the practice of dividing a customer base into groups of individuals who are similar in specific ways. Using a customer segmentation process allows companies to target and market to these groups effectively, and to also determine how to allocate their marketing resources to get the maximum results out of their marketing programs.

he definition above may be long, but try to think about this—segmenting your customers means that you are putting your customers into categories or "buckets" as I will call them. For example, if you have a group of customers and you want to do a marketing activity to promote your product or service to them, how would you divide up your customers to approach them with several different marketing message efforts? Or, if you wanted to understand which customers were bringing in the most revenues for your business, how would you divide up your customers to determine which groups were helping to bring in the most revenues? Consider the segmentation process a unique way of organizing your customer base in a way that will help you plan for marketing activities.

Remember when you were identifying your customers earlier in the book? You probably had more than one customer type, right? We will be addressing different types of customers in the segmentation exercises. The segmentation process can also help you to market and respond to your customers with greater ease. If you have an organized way of looking at your customers, you will feel better about knowing to whom you are marketing. In addition, if you can define who your customers are, you will be able to plan effective strategies that are customized to those specific customers in that category.

Knowing who your customers are is necessary for any marketing plan. Knowing your customers well is an art and takes a lot of work, but a segmentation process can make it easier to help you learn more about your customers. Consider what your current customer base looks like and how you currently organize your customers.

- Who uses the majority of your services?
- If you were to place your customers in a category or industry, what would that category be? (Is it by region, what they buy, their age group, etc.)
- What makes your customers special?

With consumer products, many companies define their customers by age group and/or by demographic area. With technology companies, customers are often divided by vertical market and/or industry. What works for your company may not work for others in terms of segmentation. The purpose of segmentation in this book will help you to understand the best way to organize your customers based on their buying behavior. Once you have completed this segmentation, you will find it easy to gather information you need and continue to monitor and track how your customers are responding to your marketing efforts in the future. You will also make better decisions on how to send marketing messages, since you will know more about your potential customers.

For this next set of exercises, you will start looking at your customers in terms of market segments. This will help you in the future as you start to determine whether certain markets are growing and why they may not be growing. If you don't happen to know the information for this next exercise, don't worry. You can do some more research later on for your customers and evaluate what types of industries they are in. If you're a small company, no doubt you can count the types of customers you have off the top of your head and easily identify what categories and/or industries they fall into.

EXERCISE 6: Segmenting Your Customers or "Bucketing Your Customers"

In this exercise, you will segment your customers and determine what your ideal customer segmentation would look like.

An Example: NowMy Networks

In the previous chapter, we discussed NowMy Networks and learned that their target audience is the small-business owner. They completed the exercises in order to segment their customers, and they picked industry specialties as a way to organize the customers they had. From their target market exercise, we learned that the company's focus is primarily to business owners, IT managers, and CFOs Read below to see how they answered the segmentation questions and then follow their example as you do the exercise using your own company.

NowMy Networks Answers to Exercise 6

NowMy Networks used the exercise to bucket their customers, and here's how they answered the questions:

How many customers does your company currently have?

We have ninety customers right now who are buying and using

our service. From a segmentation perspective, the customers group

in the following industries in terms of percentages:

60% Medical

10% Biotech

20% Semiconductor

10% Consumer Retail Businesses

0% New Market Opportunity/Customer Segment

From this exercise, we can find that the majority of their customers fall into the medical industry, with some biotech and semiconductor and consumer retail. Clearly, their medical customers are dominating their customer database.

Segmenting Your Customers with a "Customer Bucket Wish List"

Where would you like to see your segmentation?

After they did the segmentation exercise, we asked NowMy Networks what they would like to see change in their segmentation. So if they had a wish list, what would it look like? From the way that they answered the question, the company is looking to focus on the growth of the Biotech sector.

List out what segmentation percentages you would like to see! Customer Bucket Wish List:

40% Biotech

60% Medical

Note which industry you would prefer to grow or dominate.

When asked what industry NowMy Networks would prefer to grow and dominate they said that Biotech was their choice. NowMy Networks believes that Biotech would be a great market segment for them to grow and dominate; it is a big business with larger revenue potential. Also, any growing startup companies that plan to have an Initial Public Offering (IPO) within a year or two would be ideal for NowMy Networks. This would give them an opportunity to own the entire IT business from these types of companies.

What segment listed above would you consider as new opportunity market segments that can grow and why?

For NowMy Networks, the semiconductor and biotech market segments have growth opportunities. As for their greatest new opportunity market segment, the medical sector has tremendous growth opportunities. NowMy Networks is in a unique position in that they know the IT applications that are supported and needed in medical companies. Knowing about software for the biotech and medical sector is extremely valuable and hard to find from an IT company. Few IT companies truly understand what is needed in terms of software and hardware in the medical sector. This allows NowMy Networks to be perceived as a knowledgeable one-stop shop for the medical and biotech customers out there.

EXERCISE 6: Prioritizing Your Customer Segments

Now that you have recorded your customers by segment, let's go through a few steps to help you prioritize your customers in a way that will help you to make some solid goals for these customers in terms of marketing activities. This will help you in your marketing plan. To do these steps, refer to your customer segmentation exercise and review each segment that you've included.

Prioritizing your Customers

(Refer back to your customer segmentation exercise #6 and # 6A to complete this next exercise for your business.)

Step 1: Highest Percentage:

In looking at your customer segmentation exercise, review your customer segments. Circle the highest customer percentage and put a "1" by this number. This reflects the largest number of customers that you already service.

Step 2: Customer Growth Area:

Circle the customer percentage that reflects where you'd like to grow your business. Put a "2" next to this number.

Step 3: Low-hanging Fruit Growth Opportunity:

Finally, look at the customer segment where you think you have the most opportunity to both grow right now and take action with some marketing efforts in the next ninety days. As to opportunity, I mean where you can effectively focus your energies with programs and efforts to help generate more sales from this area. This could also be considered a "low hanging fruit" customer segment area ("low hanging fruit" meaning the "easiest thing to pursue next") and would be considered an easy way for you to continue producing more revenues. Your "low-hanging fruit" number is "3."

Step 4: Leveraging Work with Existing Customers:

Look at the customer segment where you feel that you've already done a majority of your marketing work. Put a "4" by this number. This can also reflect a customer segment that is already aware of your product or service and has a relatively good understanding of what you are doing as a company. If you have several segments that describe this, put the number "4" by those segments. We will also be looking at the number "4" in terms of how we can leverage some of the work that you've already done with your existing customers.

NowMy Network's Answers to Exercise 6

Let's examine how NowMy Networks answered their prioritization exercise.

> *Step 1: In step 1, they circled the medical sector as that area included the largest percentage of customers.*
>
> *Step 2: In step 2, they circled the medical sector as well, because this is the greatest growth area for their business. The medical sector is one area where they know their customers very well and receive many referrals.*
>
> *Step 3: NowMy Networks considers both the medical and biotech areas as their low-hanging fruit opportunities. They believe*

they can up-sell to current customers. Since they now have the trust of many medical device companies and physicians at this point, they find it easier to get referrals. In addition, up-selling to existing customers allows NowMy Networks to grow with their existing database of customers instead of looking for new ones. They also believe that they can grow with these customers by providing customized software that is meant only for the medical sector.

Step 4: In Step 4, NowMy Networks circled the medical area again because of all the creative relationship work they've done over the past few years getting to know these customers. They work with private medical practices, and they have spent much of their time and investment educating these physicians and medical device workers as to the realities of running an efficient and cost-saving IT department. Using analogies with them by sharing that "maintenance to the body" is parallel to "maintenance to machines," meaning that there are many needed precautions and ongoing maintenance visits that keep machines up and running, similar to the way a human takes care of their body.

YOUR TURN: Exercise 6

Now it's your turn to bucket your customers. This is a perfect exercise for you to start organizing the type of customers you do have and what type of customers you'd truly like to have.

Describe how many customers you now have, and then segment them in terms of the industry or category that makes most sense to you. Where do your customers fall in terms of segmentation? Try to identify what industry they fall into, and if you know how many customers you have right now, think of them in terms of what percentage of your business they capture. Also consider what attributes distinguish your customers from one another. For example, is it age group, industry specialty, or maybe the type of service they need? Do they typically fall into a specific age group or industry? Record how many customers you now have; segment them by their industry and indicate what percentage of your customers fall into the categories.

1. I have X number of my customers right now buying my product or service.

2. From a segmentation perspective, my customers fall into the following industries (or categories) in terms of percentages. (Should add up to 100 percent.)

----% Industry or category here

---% Industry or category here

---% Industry or category here

---% Industry or category here

---% New Market Opportunity/Customer Segment

Segmenting Your Customers with a "Customer Bucket Wish List"

In what categories would you like to see your segmentation? What would "an ideal" customer segmentation look like for your business? We will call your "ideal" customer segmentation list a "Customer Bucket Wish List." What does your "customer bucket wish list" look like?

Thinking about attracting a certain type of customer, but don't yet have them as a customer? You can still include them in this exercise. There is room for a customer that you'd like to include in your segmentation (if needed). In this exercise, first list out your current customers and the segmentation that exists in the present. Then, project your ideal segmentation and be certain to include any new industries that you are striving to enter. Not yet into that customer market? Go ahead and mark zero percentage for now. For example, if you intend to go into the financial services area, but you don't yet have any customers in that area, project the amount of your future percentage "pie" you want to have. This is your "Customer Wish List," so you can include any new market that attracts you. Because, yes, it's a "wish List!"

List out what segmentation percentages you would like to see!

Customer Bucket Wish List (should add up to 100%)

%_____

%_____

%_____

%_____

Note in what industry you would prefer to grow or dominate.

At what percentage would you consider to be new opportunity market segments that can grow and why?

Summary of your Customer Prioritization Self-Evaluation Exercise

Step 1: List out what you circled for your highest percentage customer

Step 2: List out what you circled for your Customer Growth Areas

Step 3: List out what you circled for your Low-Hanging Fruit Opportunity

Step 4: List out what you listed for Leveraging Existing Customer Work

Key Findings

What percentages did you list out for steps two and three—your greatest growth company and low-hanging fruit opportunities? These two numbers from your exercise above will prove to be very valuable during your marketing plan, so keep those customer segments at the top of your mind as you continue reading. Remember what your customer wish list segmentation looks like, as well, as you can use this to help you get closer to what types of percentages you'd ideally like to see in the future.

Think about which segments you'd like to grow in your business because we are going to focus on this in your marketing plan. If you have a low customer percentage that you'd like to grow, this is good. There are some things that you can leverage now with your existing customers that will help you to grow that customer segment. Don't be put off by low customer percentage numbers. The good thing is that you are taking a look at your customers and evaluating where and why you have customers in this area.

Reflection

NowMy Networks believes that they have become the "experts" in the IT field with respect to medical software, and because of this expertise, they believe that they can grow this area even further. Instead of searching for new customer segments, they can expand and grow the existing one by convincing them to use more of their products and services. This will definitely mean less hard work and will require fewer of their resources in order to gain more additional revenues.

With biotech companies being at the forefront of what's new and hot in technology companies, NowMy Networks is certainly on the cutting edge of revenue opportunities if they continue to go after this type of customer. Many biotech companies in Northern California are swiftly growing and expanding, offering unique IPO opportunities and acquisitions. Since NowMy Networks listed biotech on their customer wish list, this is one area where they can and will take action in terms of finding and generating new customers and revenue opportunities. Although biotech companies can be complex in their product offerings, NowMy Networks may be at an advantage since they are already familiar with the medical sector. Biotech companies are looking for people who really understand their products and processes. NowMy Networks is definitely capable of doing this because they have already learned from getting to know their medical sector customers very well. For NowMy Networks, their process for understanding a medical company's business has many similarities as they assess the challenges of working with a new biotech customer. For example, the IT systems needed to successfully run a biotech firm are very similar to the IT systems needed for a medical firm.

!———————Reflection Exercise

Return to your answers for this set of exercises. How did you circle steps one, two, three, and four? What can you now do with your low-hanging fruit opportunities to increase your revenues? Looking at the work you've already done with existing customers, and your low-hanging fruit opportunities, what goals can you set for yourself today that can help you get closer to your Customer Wish List?

What do you think are the biggest market opportunities in the market segments you listed above and why?

Chapter
11

Determine Which Segment You Want to Grow

*Which segment would you like to grow
and where would it be easiest for you to grow? In your
opinion, where is the biggest growth opportunity within the
customer segments from chapter 10? Where do you think you
can market effectively and have the most impact?*

W hen it is time for you to actually grow a customer segment, you have many possibilities. Growth can happen organically, or it can happen through acquisitions, partnering, or even through sales and marketing. What you must remember when growing a particular segment for your company, you must focus on areas that can give you the most potential for new revenues.

Your best way to grow is with your existing customers. Companies forget to consider that the best opportunity for growth is from their existing customer base. It's very simple, actually. Having worked hard to find your existing customers, chances are you know them quite well, and certainly you can find ways to grow them. If you have ideas for a quick-growing customer segment, I suggest that you focus and aggressively market to that customer area. Something may be happening right now in the economy creating a customer segment ready for marketing and growth. Sometimes, companies have great success capitalizing on a wave of popularity or trend that gives them the advantage of getting more customers. If this is the case for your company, ride that wave! For example, the growing concern for global warming trends has opened the doors for many new businesses that make "green" products. Many new mothers today are looking for organic products for their babies and are concerned about the environment. Baby products that have the ability to recycle and are earth-friendly are very popular today.

Global warming and energy conservation is a great example of how our need to care for the environment has pushed a topic to the forefront and has expanded new business growth. Today, it's hard not to go to a bookstore or read a newspaper without some new report on how global warming is affecting our planet. People are curious about global warming and many people feel a responsibility to actually make a change for the better by conserving energy and gas or finding ways to recycle. All this media attention, products, and services helping protect the environment are hot in the market right now. Service companies that can help consumers save energy and enlighten them to becoming "green" are attractive to consumers. The growth in the solar panel industry is a good example of new market growth resulting from attention on global warming and energy conservation. Right now, solar panel companies are experiencing a big boost in sales! In Northern California alone, there has been a surge of interest in solar panel companies and contractors that can improve homes to become more "green." Solar panel companies and housing development companies creating and developing energy-savers are definitely seeing an increase in their customer base in the San Francisco Bay Area because of this new trend. New customers are calling for estimates to have these solar panels installed in their businesses and residential homes. Existing solar panel customers are also looking for new ways to save even more energy in their new push for a "greener" lifestyle.

As we discussed in the previous chapter, growth opportunities can come easily to you from your existing customer base. NowMy Networks recognized that their biggest growth opportunity also happened to be their lowest hanging fruit opportunity. Since the employees and the founder are most aware of the medical sector, it's easiest for them to grow and nourish that market since they know those customers so well. They also understand that becoming the medical "IT experts" gives them the potential of becoming the leaders in this niche space. Since referrals give them a majority of their business, a bit more marketing toward medical and biotech customers should help them to get the growth they are looking to have in the next couple of years.

With your business, you may find that after the work you've done in the previous chapter, your low-hanging fruit customer may become your greatest growth opportunity. Also, many companies find that growing with existing customers is easier than finding new ones. Sometimes, the greatest increases in revenues can come from existing customers, not new customers. Although, finding a big new customer is a great way to get new revenue streams coming to your business, and landing a big new customer is always exciting and good for business.

EXERCISE 7: Determine Which Customer Segment Has the Potential to Grow the Fastest

In this exercise, you will identify which customer segment provides the greatest opportunity to grow the fastest for your business.

An Example: NowMy Networks

From the exercises we've done above, we know that NowMy Networks has found that the medical and biotech sector have given them the greatest growth opportunities. They also believe they can sell their existing customers more services and support. Read how they answered this next set of questions and then think about your business and determine how you would answer them.

NowMy Network's Answers to Exercise 7

Determine Which Customer Segment Has the Potential to Grow the Fastest

Using the exercises from chapter 10 on page 115, write down the segment that you circled with number 2, your Greatest Growth Opportunity:

Medical and biotech space

State why you think this is the Greatest Growth Opportunity:

NowMy Networks' greatest growth opportunity is the medical and biotech space. This is because there is a huge potential to grow revenues in these two business segments.

Document your Low Hanging Fruit Customer Segment:

NowMy Networks' low-hanging fruit customer segments are the medical and biotech market.

What can you do in the next ninety days to grow your greatest opportunity market? (List both sales and marketing tactics and specifically what types of marketing tactics can you develop to help you do this.)

1. *From a sales perspective, NowMy Networks can continue educating customers, and offer more services and support to help them save money.*

2. *Creating white papers showing a Return on Investment (ROI) for IT services and support can help to attract new customers in the medical and biotech space. This information will show NowMy Networks' credibility and value to their customers in terms of cost savings.*

3. *Using their existing contacts in the medical space for referral and introduction to biotech companies may open doors to new biotech clients that could benefit from buying NowMy Networks' support and services.*

Your Turn: Exercise 7

Now it's your turn! Let's now turn to your business and see how you will grow your greatest opportunity segment in the exercises below.

Determine Which Customer Segment Has the Potential to Grow the Fastest

Using the exercises from chapter 10, Page 115, write the segment that you circled with a number two, your Greatest Growth Opportunity:

State why you think this is your Greatest Growth Opportunity:

Document your Low-Hanging Fruit Customer Opportunity

What do you think you can do in the next ninety days to grow your greatest opportunity market? (List both sales and marketing tactics and specifically what type of marketing tactics you might be able to develop to help you do this. Use the NowMy Networks example above if you need help with some ideas.)

    1.)

    2.)

    3.)

Reflection

Growth in your business can be both exciting and scary. Whether it's a trend in the marketplace such as global warming that can help grow your existing or new customers or a new way of thinking about an existing customer, growth can happen with a good plan of action. Once you establish which segment you'd like to grow, you can use marketing efforts to help you get where you need to go. Using marketing tactics such as developing a white paper or establishing a referral program from existing customers are examples that show how you can potentially grow a customer to bring in additional business and revenues for you.

NowMy Networks intends to bring in new business through their existing customers and contacts. Their strategy for developing new marketing pieces that show ROI and cost savings examples will provide them with a starting point to talk with new biotech clients. In addition, their medical space business contacts are incredibly valuable as they can have an opportunity to be referred to biotech clients. Their recognition and reputation as the "medical IT experts" will go a long way as they capture new clients who are looking for a group of people who can truly understand their specific market.

! ————————————Reflection Exercise

Think about your reputation and your identity with your existing customers. Are these customers who can refer you into new growth markets? What type of marketing tools can your company create to showcase what you've done for other market segments—demonstrating your value and your expertise in a positive light?

How Current Trends
Can Impact Your
Business and Influence
Your Marketing

W hat hot and current trends are affecting your product or service? Think about all the trends out there right now—there are positive trends, negative trends, and then there are even economic trends. There are trends with technology like the iPod, the iPhone, teeth whitening trends, business outsourcing trends, and trends with going "Green." Pick your trend, there are many! Trends are everywhere, and they can impact your business every day. Be aware of the trends that could influence your business and the ways your customers may be viewing your product or service. Trends can play an important part in your business and its success.

Positive Trends That Can Impact Your Marketing Efforts

Positive trends come and go, and sometimes they stay for a while. A positive trend is one trend that encourages customers to purchase your product or service because of something that is happening in the market. These trends evolve and change over time, so being aware of these trends can really help you to anticipate what your customers will do when they decide to purchase your product or service. An example of a positive trend would be the availability of current Web 2.0 technologies such as blogs, podcasting, email campaigns, and teleseminars. Many businesses are finding that these new technologies provide a more effective way to reach an increased number of potential customers through marketing efforts. I have been working with a printing company for years that is a family-owned business. With many companies choosing to cut back on their printing efforts and instead move their marketing efforts online, this particular printing company began to think about new ways to expand their business. Since businesses are beginning to rely on Web 2.0 technologies to continue their marketing efforts, the printing company saw this trend as an opportunity to not only increase revenues, but also incorporate these new technology trends into their business model. To help their customers, they now offer Web 2.0 technology marketing campaign programs as a part of their business service offerings. Their customers love it, and they have been able to attract new customers as well with their new offerings. New and potential customers see their company as a leading edge technology and printing service, offering such programs as email campaigns, teleseminars, and direct mail print campaigns that tie into Web 2.0 technologies. Their customers are also reporting back to the printing company that using new Web 2.0 technology programs have made their businesses appear much bigger and savvier. This is a good example of a company that really tapped into a current trend and changed the way they did business for the better.

Remember that positive trends can help you and your business thrive because they can make your product or service look more attractive. You can ride the positive trend waves and continue to show your customers you are adding value. You can also expand a new product service offering or start a company from a trend. Energy conservation and "going green" is really at the forefront of news right now, and many businesses have been born from this trend such as solar companies and businesses that are providing eco-friendly products. I just got a brochure the other day in the mail for a solar backpack and diaper bag for new moms! I found that product really impressive and very interesting to young mothers who are looking for ways to help the environment. Now that you've established your target audience and your customer segments, ask yourself if there are certain trends going on in the specific industries you are targeting.

Where can you find these positive trends? Look at the media for starters! Commercials, newspapers and the radio can help to provide information in addition to online publications and resources. Many current research reports appear in online newsletter publications. Analysts are also good at writing up white-paper reports on trends on specific industries. You can also Google your industry or specific area of interest and look for trend reports on products or services that you think may be related to what you are marketing and selling.

Turning Trends Into Messages That Lead to Your Product or Service

Think about what trends are out there today. What types of trends exist that could be affecting how your customers are purchasing or not purchasing your product or service? What types of materials already exist that contain trend information that you need to help sell and market your product or service better? For example, are there reports, white papers, or any recent information that could persuade your customers or potential customers to be interested in what you are marketing to them? Think about how a current trend can provide some useful information to incorporate into your messaging. It's really this simple—by mentioning or including a positive trend in your marketing message, you may have an opportunity to lead a customer right to your product or service. For example, if you have a product that may be attractive to customers who are conscientious about the environment, and you have a product that is environmentally friendly in some way, you may consider including this fact in your messaging to the customer. Or, if you provide a service to your customers and you see a trend report that shows using your type of service would enhance their lives in some way, incorporate these facts into your messages to your customers in all your communication efforts.

We've talked about positive trends. Now you may be thinking to yourself, "What happens with a negative trend that may impact a product or service?" A negative trend example would be that some children's toys manufactured overseas in Asia are being assembled with lead components. The discovery of lead in toys has forced many toy companies to recall their products to protect customers who have purchased the toys. This trend has put many toy companies in the spotlight and scrutiny of customers who are purchasing toys for children.

In addition to trends, there are a number of factors beyond your control in terms of just how successful you can be with your product or service. As a marketer, you'll need to be one step ahead of the curve and learn to anticipate any negative trends that may potentially impact your marketing activity. Since you'll be spending time and effort to market your product or service, you'll want to be sure you've carefully thought out how the market may respond to your communications. For example, if a report has recently been found in the news pointing out the negative aspects of your product or service and you choose to address the trend, you will want to point out the positive aspects of your product or service on your Website and in all your communication pieces. You may consider using some positive testimonials from customers to highlight the positive aspects that customers find when using your product or service.

What is happening in the world today that can support your marketing efforts? Think about any specific market trends that might be in favor of what you are marketing to your customers. Trends could include the following: market research data, statistics, media reports, white papers, newspaper opinion bylines, or general news you are seeing. The exercise in this chapter can help you to identify what trends could help you with your marketing.

How Is the Economy Impacting Your Customers?

The economy affects the world every day. Although the economy may not directly impact your particular business, on some level, it impacts your customers. As a result, you need to be aware of what is influencing your customer's purchasing decisions. How they behave with respect to purchasing and budgeting may have more to do with the economy and less to do with your product or service. Let's face it, what is happening on a global level can impact what happens on a domestic level, and seeing our economy change for the good or bad is something to which every business needs to be paying attention. The economy can also dictate new trends around products and services, so it's always a good time to take a look at the business environment around you.

Economic conditions can and will impact your customer's priorities in ways of which you may be unaware. Remember, your customers also have a budget. If the economy is weak, your customers may be cutting back in areas that were once very important. They will conserve, they will scrimp, and they will cut back when the economy is not favorable. They may buy things that are less expensive or of lesser value to make themselves feel better about spending. They may instead purchase products and services that make sense to their own businesses in terms of sustaining their revenues. Even when times get tough with the economy, you can still continue to make your product or service be attractive to your customers. You can do this through your marketing efforts, pricing, and staying top of mind for your customers. What you offer your customer as a product or service needs to continue to add value to their lives. Even if you have the greatest offering in the world, you need to keep evolving with your customer's priorities. So understanding the economy will also help you to get a grip on your messaging to your customers.

Think about what's happening in the economy today and how it might be affecting your revenues. Is your product or service in a favorable light—considering the economic conditions today? If not, your marketing efforts will need to be aggressive to balance what is happening in the marketplace.

Exercise 8: Trend Analysis

In this exercise, you will identify key trends or conditions that may be impacting your product or service.

An Example: P & A HR Consulting

According to research reports from Adminstaff (the nation's leading professional employer organization offering full-service human resources services for small and medium-sized businesses) and Society of Human Resource Management (SHRM) publications, many companies are choosing to outsource human resource functions, such as recruitment, payroll, benefits, and training. This allows businesses to focus on their core competencies and to cut overhead costs with respect to salaries. As businesses continue to outsource HR, this is a positive trend for companies like P & A HR Consulting. P & A offers a variety of HR consulting services to their clients, including recruitment, strategic staffing, performance management, policy development, organizational development, and management coaching. In addition to their HR services, P & A offers a personal approach for solving problems. Instead of working with a larger HR consulting firm, businesses benefit from receiving consulting services with the principal of the firm, who has executive and management experience in addition to a variety of HR business practices. Clients get a "big company" brain with a "small company" personal touch.

P & A HR Consulting' Answers to Exercise 8

P & A HR Consulting has some positive HR trends demonstrated in several credible research reports that support and enhance marketing efforts. See how they answered the questions below to identify key trends that will continue to help them to showcase their services in a favorable light to various customers.

List out any trends over the past twelve months that have shown a favorable outcome for marketing your product or service:

> *1.) Yankee Group research predicts that the domestic market for HR outsourcing (outsourcing at least three human resources functions) will reach $42 billion by 2008.*
>
> *2.) Research firms indicate that market consolidation (large HR firms are consolidating) is happening at a rapid rate for HR consulting firms.*
>
> *3.) Research shows that many small and mid-sized companies think that outsourcing firms are expensive, inefficient, and impersonal to work with.*

List out any trends over the past twelve months (if any) that show some challenges for marketing your product or service:

> *Attention on the mergers/acquisitions of larger HR firms— leading companies to believe that larger HR firms may be a more attractive outsourced solution rather than working with an individual consultant.*

Detail any recent market research data that addresses your product or service. (This could be in a white-paper report, a research study from a publication, or some statistics from the media.)

> *Research reports from (Society of Human Resource Management) SHRM publications indicate that small and medium businesses are looking for a more personalized and customized approach to*

HR outsourcing. This means they are looking for a more one-on-one consulting approach to solving HR business problems.

Market Research from "Guide to HR Outsourcing 2007" from People Management indicates that companies don't want an in-house, full-time HR team. They instead prefer to outsource HR so their in-house teams can focus on more strategic corporate projects. As a result, many companies have understaffed HR departments that need additional help, making the use of an independent consultant a valuable and much needed solution.

Circle one:

There has been an increase/decrease in the demand of your product or service over the past twelve months.

Increase.

Based on my gathered research, the trends I find are favorable/not favorable (circle one) for marketing my product or service.

Favorable.

Key Findings

Any specific trends that show that customers are interested in a type of service or product are very helpful when it comes times to marketing efforts. For example, for P & A, recent HR trends described in human resource news articles have indicated that businesses are choosing to outsource some of their HR functions. This information gives P & A an advantage when they talk with customers. People in business understand the value of outsourcing HR functions because they save time and money. When meeting new prospective clients, P & A rarely has to sell the idea of outsourcing HR service, as most businesses already understand the value of receiving outsourced HR service. What the principal ends up selling the most is her expertise as an executive, with the unique ability to help executives at other organizations.

Trends from publications from SHRM and Forrester research now show that dollars being spent on HR outsourcing are on an upswing as companies continue to evaluate their Return on Investment (ROI). Businesses find they can become more efficient by outsourcing functions that could otherwise be done in-house and thus costing more employee time and budget dollars. Since some businesses require an ROI model or example before investing in an outside vendor, P & A could take an existing HR trend and perhaps create a white paper or brochure describing an ROI business model. This marketing piece could be a downloadable document available on the P & A Website or a brochure or flyer that could be emailed to current and future customers. P & A could also consider taking trends that discuss saving time and create a resourceful white-paper report that further reinforce the need for P & A's services and also show businesses that the firm understands their key objectives and needs. The white paper could be presented in person to executives when discussing new projects. The creation of these new marketing pieces from P & A may be able to help potential customers understand the value of hiring an HR consultant and can educate new customers on the types of HR services P & A can help to provide them with.

YOUR TURN: Exercise 8

Discuss what is happening with your product or service today in terms of the trends in the market. List out any economic conditions or any current relevant business trends you are aware of that may be impacting your product or service (either negatively or positively).

Trend Analysis

List out any trends over the past twelve months that have shown you a favorable outcome for marketing your product:

1.)

2.)

3.)

List out any trends over the past twelve months (if any) that have shown you some challenges for marketing this product:

1.)

2.)

3.)

Detail out any recent market research data about your product or service:

(This market research data could be found in a white-paper report, a research study from a publication, or some statistics from the media.)

There is an increase/decrease (circle one) in demand of your product or service over the past twelve months.

Based on my gathered research, the trends I am finding favorable/ not favorable (circle one) for marketing my product or service.

Reflection

P & A is benefiting from recent trends that show a definite need and preference for the outsourced HR consultant. This type of trend helps to give P & A additional opportunities for business. Businesses are finding HR outsourcing to be an effective way to gain specific HR expertise, cut overhead expenses, and free up their management staff for technical work. This trend is predicted to continue into the next decade, providing P & A many opportunities for growth. However, to really capitalize on these trends, P & A needs to demonstrate consistent leadership and value to companies through their distribution of interesting and creative effective marketing pieces that their customers will find informative. A few of these HR trends can be used effectively if the trends themselves are interesting to P & A's clients. For example, the HR trend that shows that companies are looking for a more customized and personalized HR outsourcing is a great way to interest new clients for P & A. As companies look to a more one-on-one approach to problem solving, P & A can promote the fact that the principal takes her program skills from large corporations and scales them down to meet the needs of each client. Her programs are customized to each client not tailored to meet the needs of all clients. This is something the principal should be focused upon in messages when creating and developing marketing pieces.

While one trend may be interesting to one client, another trend may be more useful for another. P & A needs to evaluate which of the trends would be most helpful for which clients. Identifying trends that are interesting to the customer will help to make P & A appear savvy and knowledgeable. If P & A can pinpoint trends that may impact their customers' businesses, they will continue to offer valuable insight and information to their customers and potential customers.

! ———————————————— **Reflection Exercise**

Do today's trends help you better market your product or service? Are there any specific trends you are seeing with respect to research, articles, or general news that you see that may impact and influence your marketing efforts? Based on the above exercises, are you aware of a strong need for your product or service today? If recent trends don't show the strong need for your product or service, do you see the opportunity and why?

What Your Competitors Are Doing and What They Are Not Doing

Some business owners become overwhelmed and fearful when they think about what their competitors are doing and how fast they are moving in on potential customers. Yes, it's savvy for you to be aware of what your competitors are saying and doing from a marketing and sales perspective, and it's always good business to know who your competitors are. But consider what your competitors may not be doing. Be proud of what your company does and the accomplishments that have made you successful. What your competitors may fail to focus on may be a golden opportunity for you. What your competitors fail to discuss with their customers might be the very thing that your customer truly needs to hear from you. If you are so new to the market that you don't yet have any competitors, consider the other companies that provide a similar type of service or product that you want to market and use them for the exercises in this chapter.

Find out what is happening out there with your competitors. When you create your marketing plan, you need to consider how your competitors are marketing their product or service. This helps you make decisions about what types of marketing activities you should pursue. Focus on your top one to three competitors or considered competitors and identify how they are marketing their product or service. Are they pushing a certain message that is attractive to customers by features in their product or service? Or are they pushing a specific value proposition? Possibly they have an incredible brand that is hard for buyers to resist. Do this research so that when you are ready to do your marketing plan, you can determine what activities are going to really make your product or service stand out. Many companies keep up to date on their competitors through market research. You can monitor how your competitors are doing by looking at their Websites and by looking at how they are positioning themselves. Also, your current customers may be well informed about your competitors and they may be willing to share this information with you. You may also get some of your ideas from looking at what your competitors are doing, and that's great too. Keep focused on how they are marketing to their customers, because chances are, your competitors' customers may potentially one day be your customers, too.

Sometimes, It's All About Perception

Understanding how to market your product or service is reflected in how you are already perceived in the marketplace. For example, if you are a small business and your product or service is already a commodity, you may be challenged to differentiate yourself from your competitors.

If your product or service is already known in the marketplace, you may already have a reputation for having a great product or giving a great service through your other customers. This is your good news! However, if people have used your product before and it needs some improvements, you will need to address any concerns that the market may have around your product or service.

Think about a customer who goes to a yellow page book to find a specific type of company. Perhaps your company is not listed but the customer finds another one instead and calls. Think about a customer that does a Google search and finds all kinds of great information about your competitor, but nothing is listed about you. Or the customer thinks your business is smaller than another business because you have no website and decides to choose your competitor over you. The point is people may be missing out on your product or service because they don't know about it or haven't heard about it before. Or, people may not have heard enough good stuff about what you are offering to take a risk to buy it. It's up to you to create a good impression and influence your customers through marketing that you have a great product or service to buy!

If your product or service is well known, do you think that your potential customers know what your company does versus your competitors? It helps to have an understanding of what you do in comparison to what your competitors do. If you need to discuss this with your customers, you can. You should be very well versed in what your customers think about what your business does versus your competitors.

Doing Market Research on Your Competitors

In some ways, talking to your customers is the best and easiest way to get information about your competitors. Who better to talk with than a customer who has maybe tried several different products and has an idea of what works and what doesn't work? Your best customer might be a former customer of your competitor. Also, in most cases, your customers have probably already done some research on companies out there that can help them and may have come across your competitors in the process.

You can tap into your customers' perspective of their awareness of the marketplace relative to competition. Survey your customers through a variety of marketing efforts. Companies are using e-newsletters and online marketing campaigns to survey customers on an ongoing basis. Your use of online mini-surveys is your opportunity to find out what makes your product or services special or what other products or services your customers use and like.

What about doing market research? Market research is only valuable if it is current and relevant to your market and target audience. Even market research very quickly becomes out of date! Budget some dollars for market research that pertains specifically to your business and your competitors. There are a number of public and private research companies that can help you find what you need. If you can't afford to do market research, have your company conduct your own online surveys and focus groups to help you get the information you need. In addition, there are a number of online survey tools (such as Zoomerang and SurveyMonkey) that are relatively inexpensive and will result in your having quick market research data from your customers.

When you decide to survey your customers to find out more about your competitors, also include what your customers like about the way they market, advertise, and promote their product or service. For example, if your competitors are great at online marketing, this is something that you want to know about! If your customers get emails every week from your competitor, and they like this, you need to make sure you take note for your own plan. If you decide to do an online survey, be sure to ask leading questions for answers about the other companies your customers may have looked at in the past. Find out what they like about your competitors or companies in your industry and how they found you. What other questions can you ask your customers about your competitors and other companies that may compete with you?

EXERCISE 9: Analyzing Your Competitor's Messaging and What's Working Well for Them

Tapping into the sales tactics of your competitors will truly help you with your marketing strategies. In this exercise, you will have the opportunity to see your competitor's strengths and find ways for you to truly be competitive.

An Example: NowMy Networks

We've used NowMyNetworks in several examples in the book. Review how they perceive their current customers and understand what they are doing from a marketing perspective.

NowMy Networks's Answers to Exercise 9

Here is how NowMy Network answered the questions for Exercise 9.

My main competitor (example: The competitor can take away market share, compete directly for same customers, etc.) is:

Our main competitors are independent IT Consultants and very small IT firms as they are "break/fix-it guys" who fix your

IT problems for $50 an hour or less. Your problem will be solved, temporarily. However their lack of experience and their inability to solve the core problems results in a band-aid solution.

My customers have the following perception of my top competitor (list main attributes like fast service, performance, friendly service, etc.)

NowMy Networks customers think that independent IT consultants are inexpensive and that these consultants quickly fix a problem. These consultants don't take the time to educate the customer about the real problem and they do not know how to help the customers increase their sales.

From the viewpoint of my customers, what are the business issues that my competitors are addressing? How are they getting those messages out? (Email, print, direct mail, Website, sales training, seminars, etc.)

NowMy Network's competitors address the needs of customers by providing a quick, fast-turn service. They get their messages out through the Yellow Pages advertisements that go to small businesses. This is effective for the competitor.

List out the three things that your competitor is doing well in your opinion in terms of their marketing efforts:

1) *Noticeable advertisements in Yellow Pages where small-business owners look.*

2) *Frequency of advertisements in publications and online Websites where small-business owners look for resources.*

3) *Marketing/advertising in a manner that appears to be low-cost*

*to companies so that customers can "get in the door" quickly
and get the service.*

What value messages are your competitors using to address their
customer business issues today?

1) *Fast service*

2) *Low cost at a value*

3) *Fixing your computer/IT needs without hassle.*

In what three areas of business does my product or service provide what
my competitors do not?

1.) *NowMy Networks knows their software and they are experts at
what they do.*

2.) *Helping small businesses increase their sales through IT
solutions*

3.) *Ability to lease out a solution, not just a "break/fix service."
Offering IT as a service AND a solution for your software
and hardware. Once any problems are resolved, we continue
to provide you with long-term solutions.*

YOUR TURN: Exercise 9

Now it's your turn to do the exercise. Consider your competitor(s)
and your business, and do the exercise below. Use the NowMy Networks
example above for reference, if you need to.

My main competitor (example: The competitor can take away market
share or compete directly for same customers, etc.) is:

My customers have the following perception of my top competitor (list main attributes like fast service, performance, friendly service, etc.):

In the eyes of customers, what are the business issues that my competitors are addressing? In what manner are they getting out those messages? (Email, print, direct mail, Website, sales training, seminars, etc.)

In your opinion, list out the three areas that your competitor is doing well in terms of marketing efforts:

1.)
2.)
3.)

What value messages are your competitors using to address customer business issues (such as cost savings, best performance, best quality, etc.) today?

What three business solutions does my product or service provide that my competitors are not addressing?

1.)
2.)
3.)

Reflection

In reviewing the exercise above, NowMy Networks has learned that their competitors were clever at identifying their customer's main pain points which is IT help. NowMy Networks' competitors are already using their own messages heavily in their marketing and advertising messages. They are using Yellow Page ads where small-business owners tend to look for solutions. Yet, what their competitors don't do is offer a complete solution, and they also don't talk about providing a service that provides ongoing support and service for the long term. This is an opportunity for NowMy Networks to do what their competitors do not do. For every customer wanting a quick "break/fix" IT solution, there will be another customer who will want a quick solution providing efficient long-term solutions.

! ——————————————————— Reflection Exercise

What are your competitors "saying" in their advertising and marketing? What are they not saying? Where can you differentiate yourself from your competitors and show your product or service in a more attractive light compared to your competitors? Review what your competitors do well in terms of their current marketing efforts. Learn from what they are doing well! In what way can you improve your marketing efforts by watching your competitors?

How Revenues
Can Impact Your Plan

nderstanding how your revenues work today can really help your marketing plan in the future. When I say revenues, I mean the income generated from your current business. Does your business have financial objectives? Do your marketing objectives help to meet those financial goals for your company? Let's focus on your finances so you are clear about what is happening financially with your business. This is really going to help with your marketing plan in a number of ways. If you can understand what is happening with your revenues today, you can set clear objectives for the future and determine how you can continue to increase your revenues.

If you cringe when you think of numbers, relax. We won't be crunching numbers and setting up macro formulas here in your marketing plan. However, we will evaluate the main source of your income and explore new customer target areas based on your current successes, and find areas in which you don't want to invest. Once you look at your revenues, it will be much easier to determine what you should and shouldn't be doing with marketing activities.

Tracking Your Revenues Quarterly

How do you currently track your revenues: quarterly or annually? In order to continue marketing your business effectively, you must understand where your revenues are coming from. It's a good idea to check in with your revenues quarterly in addition to annually. Are they consistent? Do you know what your cash flow looks like on a quarterly basis? If you don't track your revenues quarterly, you may want to begin doing this.

If you are a consultant or a small-business owner, understanding your revenues will be a fairly simple task. In fact you may know this off the top of your head. You may even be able to rattle off the reason your revenues are up or down because you are very much involved and impacted by those numbers. Whether you do or don't know your revenues off the top of your head, you should do the exercises in this chapter anyway. You'll want to know where your revenues are coming in based on your customer segmentation. Understanding this will help you grow those areas of your business that need additional revenues.

Revenue Growth Rates: What is the Trend?

Many factors may influence how and why your revenues look the way they do. For example, there may be certain industries that are more interested in your product or service. To make your marketing plan more comprehensive, you will want to plan ahead for any changes that may impact your revenues. For example, if one of your largest customers is planning to expand their business and your product or service, this may impact your revenues if they continue to purchase from you. Understanding these conditions can help you to plan your marketing efforts accordingly.

Do you notice any patterns or trends in growth or decline rates in your revenues? Do you see your revenues decline at a certain time of the year? Documenting these patterns and changes can help you in the future as you spend money on marketing activities and allow you and your business to stay flexible. There will be ups and downs during growth rates in your business so you want to stay prepared. Use the next exercise as a template to understand what's happening with your revenues.

EXERCISE 10: Revenue Snapshot and Analysis

In this exercise, you will have an opportunity to learn what is driving your revenues and analyze how your revenues are performing from a quarterly and annual basis. You will also determine if they are increasing or decreasing and why.

An Example: NowMy Networks

When NowMy Networks did their revenue snapshot and analysis exercise, the medical sector was shown to be bringing in the most money for their business. The medical sector was obviously the strength customer in their segmentation exercises in previous chapters. What did they learn from doing the revenue analysis exercises? By doing the analysis work, they found that their business grew in revenues from one year, corresponding to their increase in technology clients. They also had hired new resources to help with the business development and sales side of the business. The new customers warranted their hiring more help in their business. Having more people marketing to their business helped their revenues to grow! They realized that when dedicated resources were applied to the business, their revenues had the potential to increase. These examples show you that after you have completed your own business analysis work on your revenues, you may have a better understanding for what is needed to increase your own revenues.

NowMy Network's Answers to Exercise 10

Name of your business

NowMy Networks

What does your business provide?

Managed Information Technology (IT) Services, Solution Provider

How it helps your clients:

IT solutions for small businesses

Increasing their sales

What are your annual revenues?

$1.5M

What are your quarterly revenues (if known)?

$450K

Next, NowMy Networks evaluated the source of their revenues with respect to their customer segments. Then they assessed which customers were increasing and which were declining.

On a quarterly basis, our revenues are coming from the following market segments:

65% medical

35% other (biotech, retail, semiconductor)

Write down your revenue by customer segment and percentage:

60% Medical

20% Semiconductor

10% Biotech

10% Consumer/Retail

After doing this exercise, which customer segments bring in the most revenue for you?

Medical

Examine your revenues for the year and calculate an average growth rate from the previous year. (If your business is too new to compare previous annual year numbers, use quarterly numbers only.)

Revenue Growth Rates: Are they increasing or declining?

Document your revenues for the year and your growth rate (if known).

For example: 2007 revenues were at $1,500,000. This shows a growth of 10% compared to previous year 2006 revenues of $90,000.

Annual Growth Rate: 10%

Decline Rate: 0%

What factors have contributed to any changes in your revenues this year? Indicate either a decline or increase in revenues.

Revenues for NowMy Networks have increased this year by 10%. Here are some factors that have contributed:

1.) Up-selling to existing customers

2.) Hiring more employees has allowed dedicated marketing and sales resources to talk with more potential customers, thereby giving more contracts a "quick close."

Which customer segments are growing in revenues and which are declining?

Customer Segments that are growing include:

Medical

Customer Segments that are declining include:

Retail

Key Findings

NowMy Networks has increased their technology customers. In fact, they have doubled their technology customers and have increased revenues. Their medical revenues are increasing as they produce better contracts with their medical companies. An area that is declining is retail/consumer. This is not a skill area for NowMy Networks. NowMy Networks doesn't see the retail/consumer business as a revenue generator since they don't want to invest the time to become more skilled with this type of customer. In the future, they may decide not to focus at all on this retail/consumer area.

YOUR TURN: Exercise 10

Examine and gather your revenue information and complete the exercise below. Reference the NowMy Networks example for guidance for filling out the questions.

Revenue Snapshot

Enter the name of your business:

Enter what your business does:

How does it help your clients?

Enter your annual revenues:

Enter your quarterly revenues (if known):

Evaluate the main source of your revenues with respect to your customer segments. Then, determine which customer segments are growing and which are declining.

On a quarterly basis, my revenues are coming from the following market segments

Enter your revenue by customer segment:

_____%

_____%

_____%

After doing this exercise, which customer segments are bringing in the most revenue for you?

Let's look at your growth rates in terms of revenues and see whether they are increasing or declining. Determine the reasons that made these numbers increase or decline in your business.

Revenue Growth Rates: Are they increasing or declining?

Examine your revenues for the year and calculate an average growth rate from the previous year. (If your business is too new for you to compare previous annual year numbers, only use quarterly numbers.)

Document your revenues for the year and your growth rate (if known).

For example: 2007 revenues were at $1,500,000. This shows a growth rate of 10% compared to previous year 2006 revenues of $ 90,000.

Annual Growth Rate: %

Decline Rate: %

Check in with yourself for a moment. Did your revenues grow or decrease in the past year? Do you see your revenues trending upward and where? Do you know the reasons for this?

What factors have contributed to any changes in your revenues this year? Detail out some factors that may have contributed to any changes in revenues:

1.)

2.)

Examine your customer segments to find which are growing and bringing in additional revenues and which are declining and bringing in fewer revenues than the previous year.

Which customer segments are growing in revenues and which are declining?

Customer segments that are growing include:

Customer segments that are declining include:

Understanding What Impacts Your Revenues Today

Take a look at where you are getting the majority of your revenues in the exercises above. Is it from one specific industry? Is it several? Think about how you were able to achieve those revenues in that particular industry segment. Was it targeted or just something that you fell into? Maybe it could be because of your expertise. Many companies find that the industry where they are making the most money is often times the easiest industry and the most accessible. This is great news, but part of marketing is actually continuing to bring attention to those customers that are accessible and also bringing new customers to the attention of your product or service that may not be so accessible.

Take a look at where you are getting the most traction in terms of revenues per market segment or industry. Then look at the lowest revenue industry percentage. Do you want to grow this area or get rid of it? If your plan is to grow your revenues in a specific target area or industry, you're going to want to look at what you've done so far in terms of your success rate. Have you done any marketing at all? If not, what will it take to get you to the next level of success with that segment? This is what you will want to address in your marketing plan. If you are trying to grow a new segment entirely, you will definitely want to pay particular attention to market research and of course market trends to help you determine what the best course of action will be for your marketing efforts in this new area. However, be forewarned; marketing in an entirely new segment will require you to do some extensive market research first to determine how you will reach your target audience in the best possible way.

Reflection

When NowMy Networks did their revenue exercises, they recognized that their revenues had increased from the previous year due to an increase in technology clients and an increase in dedicated marketing and sales resources. More dedicated resources translated into more customer sales for NowMy Networks. As more marketing and sales people became dedicated resources to their customers, revenues began to increase. Their business is growing, and as they make an effort to know their medical customers even better, they will continue to grow. Revenues are also in an upswing in the areas of the business that they want to grow. This is an ideal situation and they need to continue tracking their growth rates on a quarterly and annual basis to ensure that their medical segment revenues continue to grow.

Reflection Exercise

Assess the results of your customer segments. Are your revenues increasing in the areas that you want them to be? Is it obvious why some segments are declining and why some are increasing? What has contributed to those numbers? Summarize any conditions that positively affect your increasing revenues and help you to increase revenues in other areas. Conversely, summarize any conditions that negatively impact your opportunity for revenues.

Chapter
15

What Is Your Business Doing Right Today?

You've done groundbreaking work by examining your business and the various aspects where it is well run. We've examined your core business offering, your customer segments, your target audience, your customer lens, your revenues, your target audience and more. All are important, but so is taking a step back and considering your business today. Where is it headed? Are you growing, is your product or service growing, or are you just launching? You may be just starting your business. A number of things are working well for your business and are helping you to succeed at various levels. Obviously, there will be areas in your business that will also need improvement. Before you do your marketing plan, it is important that you know where you are now. Some things that you do in your business may be working really well for you and are easy for you. These are the types of business factors that can help you to continue your successes in the future.

Let's look at your business right now in "real time." When I say "real time" I mean this minute, this day, this month. Doing this will help you understand what is happening with your product or service and will help you to identify what strengths and weaknesses to address in your marketing plan. The evaluation that you do for this exercise can be used repetitively on a quarterly basis. You may decide to do this exercise every ninety days—continuing to monitor your marketing activities and to ensure that you meet objectives.

What Is Working Well for You in Your Business?

What's happening right now in terms of your revenues? How are you currently marketing your product or service? Have your current marketing efforts impacted your company in a positive way? In your opinion, what is right about your business? What is going well?

What are three things that are working well for your business and why? Are you marketing a unique product that is appealing to customers? Do you have a strong engineering team that has developed a good prototype? Are revenues increasing year after year? Do you develop strong relationships with your customers and continue to work with them? People may truly like your product, or maybe your sales force is so experienced and can sell just about anything to anyone. Evaluate these good things and write them down. The purpose of this next exercise is simple—find out what is working well. Chances are, once you identify what is working well in your business, you may also find that you have not been considering these factors in your current marketing efforts to customers.

EXERCISE 11: What Is Working Well in Your Business Today?

In this exercise you will identify what is working well in your business and marketing activities. Understanding what is working well now will give you a good perspective on what can be done to further market your product or service.

An Example: P & A HR Consulting

As a small HR management services firm, P & A offers a variety of HR consulting services to their clients. Services include recruitment, "strategic staffing," organizational development, performance management and management coaching, as well as HR policy development and implementation. P & A has also been very successful servicing a number of financial services firms and non-profit organizations. In fact, serving non-profit organizations seems to be a new specialty for P & A. Read the exercise below and find out what's working well for P & A. Learn how what is working well for them can really help them to sell even more of their business services.

P & A's Answers to Exercise 11

List the three things that are working well in your business:

1.) 80% of P & A Business clients come from referral relationships.

2.) Pro-bono work for non-profits has led to a surge of new clients.

3.) P & A has successfully taken large human resources management programs and scaled them down for small companies, which has been a benefit for P & A's target audience.

List out the types of marketing activities that have been working well for your business: an advertisement, your Website, a promotional piece or marketing piece that you give to customers. It could also be something as simple as your outbound telemarketing calls to potential customers:

1.) *Eighty percent of P & A's clients are coming from referrals: relationships from the owner's prior employers, associates, and senior management team members. Each referral has been a rich source of new business to P &A. Since referrals work well for P&A, it would be smart and productive if she used these sources for testimonials and references in her marketing pieces or proposals or in meetings with potential new clients.*

2.) *The Principal at P & A has had great success with doing pro-bono work for a non-profit organization. As a result of the pro-bono work, the principal of the firm has been able to gain both insights and experience working with non-profits and their boards and can relate and apply this knowledge and experience to other non-profit organizations.*

For example, building on her experience working with the Executive Director and CEO on human resource issues in one organization, she can apply that expertise to other non-profit organizations. P&A's clientele now consists of several non-profits in the health and human services area, specifically relating to children and women's issues; some of that is due to her past experience, but some new work can be directly attributed to the experience she gained doing pro-bono work.

3.) *P & A's principal is expert at taking sophisticated human resources and performance management programs that have worked for larger organizations and scaling these programs down to work for smaller organizations and for non-profits.*

The availability of these programs for small businesses is invaluable. P & A's principal can continue to market these systems and programs to small businesses who are looking for "big business expertise" but need a program that is tailored to their specific business at a cost they can afford.

Key Learnings

The principal at P & A has experience working with large companies and has many business contacts. Her contacts have been a great source of referrals for her, bringing her much new business. Since using referrals tends to work for her, and her referrals are comfortable giving her positive references to other clients, a good recommendation for the future would be to have P & A include some of those referrals in brochures, on a Website, and in any sales or marketing communications literature mailings.

The principal of P & A has a tremendous amount of experience working for Fortune 500 companies although her current target audience is small businesses. She is skilled in taking the processes and HR programs from large organizations and scaling them down to an efficient system for use with a small business. Small businesses are happy to find that P & A can give this kind of work. Showcasing her unique skill is a good way for her to gain even more clients.

Learning to Incorporate What's Working Well into Marketing Efforts

The information that's been gathered from these exercises can be incredibly valuable to a business owner for planning new marketing activities. Remember that when asked what was working well for P & A, the exercises showed that referrals, pro-bono non-profit work, and large programs scaled for smaller organizations were P & A's tactics that worked well for the business.

However, P & A doesn't mention any of this in her current marketing literature or proposal information. Instead, the principal of the company focuses on her capabilities and solutions. Mentioning P & A's ability to scale to small organizations may provide her with more opportunities with additional smaller organizations that need her skills and expertise.

Learning from these exercises, the principal of the firm has decided to include referrals as testimonials in her marketing materials and has a plan to promote a list of the non-profit companies with whom she has worked. In addition, she has a new program idea to promote her skills of creating specialized small-business HR programs. Her idea includes giving her programs a marketing brand campaign and a name and adding a business model that will be approachable and attractive to her small business clients. The launch of the program will be introduced later this year on her Website and in her new marketing literature. To further her success in the non-profit arena, she plans to target her new program to non-profits and other small businesses. She will use her new materials to promote her business to her referral network and to members of professional organizations with whom she is associated.

Learning to Create More Success with the information Gathered

The P & A principal was really interested in working with non-profits when the business first began. To gain more non-profit experience, she offered her services by doing some pro-bono work for an organization in which she was interested. After completing pro-bono projects, she gained expertise in the non-profit area, and she also earned credibility from the types of organizations with whom she wanted to work.

While doing her pro-bono work, she noticed that non-profits had similar organizational development issues that were found in larger for-profit companies, but they lacked the resources to address their issues. She applied her professional expertise to these issues and assisted them in resolving issues and in the process helped them train their managers. These successful experiences gave her business credibility with businesses in the non-profit arena, and she was able to sign new contracts with other organizations. Non-profits appreciate both her non-profit and corporate experience. Today she sits on the board of the non-profit where she did pro-bono work, increasing her credibility to the non-profit arena.

Taking what was working well for her a step further proved to be a good strategic move for her organization. Today, in addition to her for-profit clients, she works with more than four non-profit organizations, enjoys the work, and feels satisfied about how she gives back to her community.

YOUR TURN: Exercise 11

Think about your business and record what you believe are the top three things that are working very well in your business.

What's working well in my business?

1.)

2.)

3.)

Think about everything that is working well. In your opinion, how can these three items listed above help to further enhance the marketing of your product or service? Could you tell your customers about what you listed above and find ways to promote some of these positive factors in your marketing messages? An example would be promoting your product's features in your marketing messages and campaigns or speaking to your potential customers about what is working well for your existing customers.

How can what's working well in your business help your product or service? Write down how what's working well in your business can help you to further market your product or service.

1.)

2.)

3.)

Reflection

The exercise above shows clearly that P & A has much that is working well and that can be described in their marketing efforts. The non-profit experiences should be emphasized, and the successes from their most current projects will bring in more non-profit clients. In addition, small businesses looking for a customized HR program have the benefit of working with someone who can easily scale down to their needs. From a reputation and credibility standpoint, P & A can also use her non-profit business contacts and referrals to help secure relationships with new clients. Most importantly, by learning from the non-profit pro-bono work, the principal of P & A deepened her expertise working with non-profits, expanded her services reach, and as a result, can now offer more specific and tailored HR solutions to more clients.

Reflection Exercise

What are the three areas that are working well for your business right now? Have you been able to demonstrate what is working well with potential customers? What efforts can you make to take the things that are working well a step further, to help you market your product or service even better? For example, can you build on your expertise in one area of your business to expand and grow another? Using the knowledge you have about what's working well in your business, can you think of some steps you can take to create more future successes for your business?

PART III

Developing Your Marketing Plan

IN PART III, YOU WILL find and use a marketing demand tool template that ranks your product or service in terms of customer demand. Once you have established your company's product or service ranking using the marketing demand tool template, you will receive best practices and tips for marketing activities that apply to your business based on where your business lies in the demand tool. These marketing activities should be considered when you pursue your marketing plan efforts. Complete the marketing demand tool template before you use the marketing plan template in Chapter 17.

Chapter 16

Using the Marketing Demand Tool

Y ou've done a lot of great work already, but before we dive into the marketing plan template, I'd like you to first take a look at this really easy tool to get you thinking about what types of marketing activities might be best for your business. Before we figure out what types of marketing activities might be good for you, we'll first evaluate where your business is in relationship to customer demand. What do I mean by customer demand? The customer's need and want for your product or service!

Planning Marketing Tactics by Identifying where your product or service ranks

There are a number of marketing tactics to choose from when it comes time to plan for your product or service. The possibilities are endless. Yet, you want to select the right marketing efforts for you and your business and it sure helps if you invest in the right marketing activities. One way to do this effectively is to first identify where your product or service sits in terms of demand. Simply put, what's the demand for what you are selling and marketing? The marketing demand tool presented in this chapter may help you to understand just exactly where you may fit with respect to your product or service. Each color on the demand tool represents a position of demand for your product or service. You will use this tool to identify where you believe your product or service fits into one of the four quadrants and then follow the marketing suggestions for that placement.

The marketing demand tool can help you to evaluate your product or service in terms of the customer's need and/or demand. You will use the marketing demand tool to identify where you believe your product or service fits. Is it in high demand? Is it declining, increasing? By using this tool as a guide, you can benchmark where you need to address your product or service with your marketing efforts. Once you've placed your estimate as to where you are with demand for your product, put your competitor and/or partner's place on this tool graph as well. Then review the suggestions for the types of marketing activities you should think about pursuing. This will help to not only give you ideas, but to also give you some solid marketing projects that you should be considering in your ninety-day marketing plan template in chapter 17. As your business grows and changes, take notes of how the marketing tool placement that you have selected evolves over time.

When you look at the demand quadrant and find that your product is in low demand, don't worry. This is an opportunity for you to find some ways to market your product or service more effectively to customers. You may be in a unique position to create demand or need for your product or service by doing some outreach to customers through promotional programs, your website, or direct mail or advertising campaigns. If you are in high demand, you may have a number of customers to also contend with, or maybe not. If you are in high demand, you may also be scrambling to get resources to cover all the needs for your product or service. Or, demand may be increasing the presence of competitors out there in the marketplace. In any case, if the demand is high for your product or service, clearly identifying what you can do to add value is increasingly more important to your customers. Think about how important it is that you speak directly to your customers' needs if you are in high demand or low demand! In both cases, you'll really want to focus on the clarity of your message and know what you're marketing!

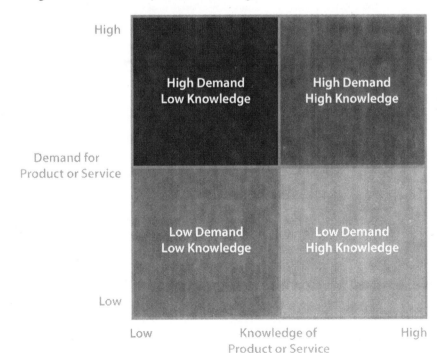

EXERCISE 12: Marketing Demand Tool Review

Review the demand tool visual above and think about the demand for your product or service. Is your product in low demand and do your customers have little knowledge of what you do? Or is your product in high demand? You may be in the middle. Try to determine where your company fits on the chart. Once you have determined where your product or service belongs on the demand tool chart, review the suggestions for marketing activities that address your position in the demand cycle of this quadrant.

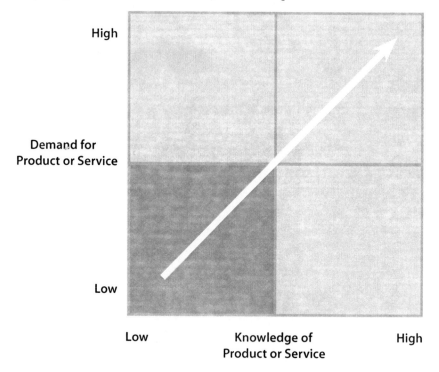

Low Demand for Product or Service: What Types of Marketing Activities Should You Pursue?

If your product or service is in low demand, there may be low awareness for your product or service. You may not yet have a market established for what you are selling and marketing. Or, economic conditions may also be a factor determining the demand of your product, so external circumstances may be driving your product to be less popular in the marketplace right now.

When you are flushing out your marketing plan, you will want to look back at where you are in the demand cycle of your product. If your product is in low demand, your marketing plan should include activities that can give you maximum coverage quickly. For example, you will want to explore and invest in activities that can give your company a lot of exposure to help drive demand. How can you maximize your marketing efforts if no one knows about your product? This is a good question. Review the following best practices to give you some helpful ideas.

What are the Best Practices for Marketing Activities with a Low-Demand Product or Service?

- **Establish product or service credibility**

   Think about your credibility first and foremost. Customers want to purchase products or services that have a reputation for providing a good service. So in saying this, you will want to develop marketing pieces with content (such as brochures, advertisements, Website, email communications, etc.) conveying you are a credible company with a good quality product or service. You can establish credibility by mentioning your current satisfied, happy customers. You can also establish credibility by showing that other credible companies use your product or service! Another way to demonstrate credibility is to show that customers need and like your product or service, and those who have used your product are willing to purchase again and again! Let your customers help you to create the demand you need to continue selling more of your product or service!

- **Strong Examples of how a problem has been solved**

    Customers will also want examples of ways your product or service has been used and will need to understand what problem has been solved. Case studies and testimonials are great ways to showcase how you are solving problems successfully. Once a case study or testimonial is written, you can print it or post it on your Website for customers and potential customers to read and download. A Customer Reference program can also help you to get your happy customers agreeing to reference your work to others. A Customer Reference program is a program that includes a person or network of people that manage customer contributions such as a case study, testimonial, success stories, product references, etc. A Customer Reference program is sometimes appropriate for service vendors so that customers can call on other customers to see their satisfaction level. Showing customers that your product or service solved a problem for another company is an excellent way to gain trust and make potential customers understand that you are capable of creating solutions that work well for other people. It also helps to show that there is demand for your product or service.

- **Continue to Drive Awareness Programs and Network! Network! Network!**

  Look to plan marketing activities that can drive awareness to potential customers about your company. Online communities are a great way to talk to people about your product or service and network at the same time. Networking is also critical. Continue to find networking opportunities that allow you to promote your product or service to a broad audience. For example, if you are marketing to CEOs at technology start-ups, begin attending seminars and conferences where you can get in front of these types of people to introduce your idea. Networking is also a great way to collect information on the types of people that can potentially become part of an advisory council for your product and help you to gain recognition in your market.

Specific Examples to consider for Marketing to a Low Demand Product or Service:

- Participate in or create an Online Community Blog
- Consider purchase of Google key ad words for your product or service
- Activities that show customers need your product (such as a marketing or advertising campaign showing a problem/solution)
- Customer Survey that becomes a credible piece such as a white paper showing how your company provided a solution. (Results from survey can become an advertorial testimonial on product or service with an advertisement, article, case study, or testimonial)

- Activities (such as a product or service award, Customer Reference program, Case Study, Advertorial, testimonial quote on satisfaction of using product, etc.) that demonstrate that satisfaction results from using your product or service

- Marketing literature that showcases your customer base and/or affiliates your product and company with other credible organizations or provides credible testimonials from customers using and liking your product.

- Clear marketing pieces such as brochures, flyers, website copy, sales presentations that convey your message in succinct, easy-to-read format. Repetitive cycles on a quarterly or monthly basis of this messaging are important.

- Awareness campaign programs that put your company in the limelight: road shows, conference speaking opportunities, articles in targeted publications, etc.

- Survey results from focus groups or customer surveys that becomes informative piece or white paper document

- Advertorials (Customer Testimonial with advertisement)

- eNewsletters

- Conference Speaking Opportunities (such as a keynote or workshop session track speaking opportunity that allows you to talk about your product or service)

- Strong Online presence (Website, newsletters, collateral)

- Sponsorship opportunities that showcase your product or service and display your logo

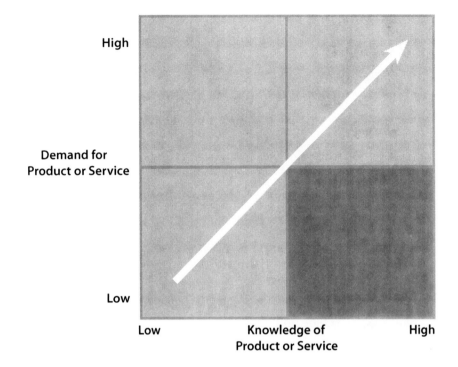

Some Demand for product or service: What Type of Marketing Activities Should You Pursue?

If there is some demand for your product or service, you should continue to create and implement marketing activities that show your product or service is a leader in the marketplace. You will also want to demonstrate that you are a successful solution for your customers. Awareness of what you are doing for your customers will be critical to getting you to your next level of growth.

What are the best practices for marketing activities with some demand for product or service?

- **Increase awareness of product or service**

    Continue to create and leverage marketing activities that show your leadership in the marketplace and increasingly provide examples of how customers are using your product or service to help their business succeed. If there is some demand for your product or service, make sure what you are marketing and selling is made known to your customers. The name of your business and what it does should appear frequently in areas where your potential customers can see and learn more about. Whether this means online, a yellow page ad, or a marketing piece, make sure your company is out there. This can be achieved through a number of marketing and advertising activities. You want to be heard and be known!

- **Show Examples of Strong Customer Satisfaction**

    Leverage what customer segments in which you have already started success and be certain to use those customers to help you get more customers. Asking customers for referrals and/or references is a great way to validate that your customers are happy. Keep a log of customers who are offering their support so that you can turn those successes into marketable pieces such as white papers and testimonials that can help show that your company provides good service and that customers are happy!

- **Demonstrate Your Value To Customers**

    Marketing pieces that continue to demonstrate your value to your customers will bring you closer to driving demand for your product or service. Use strong examples of how you demonstrate value to your customers and why they keep coming back for more. You can do this through talking about your product or service and how it makes the lives of your current customers better. You can also do this by giving examples of how your product or service is liked and used by your current customers. So what types of activities should be considered if your product or service has some demand in the market?

Specific examples of marketing activities to consider for marketing to a product or service with some demand include:

- Online newsletters, webinars (live visual and audio online presentations available for your customers), podcasts
- Purchase Google key ad words for your product or service
- Media articles, placements, and write-ups in publications that your customers would read
- Awards for your product or service that would make your business stand apart
- Increasing online outreach and promotion on your website, outreach to your customers through surveys, etc....
- Branding activities such as new logo and look/feel for your Website, creating more awareness to customers
- Research reports featuring your product or service being used by customers
- White papers highlighting specific features and/or testimonials about using your product or service
- Attend relevant conferences where your customers will visit to get information on your product or service
- Speaking opportunities such as at a conference or workshop where you can talk about your product or service
- E-newsletters that you can create and distribute to your current and potential customers
- Customer Reference programs that allow you to highlight customers that favor your product or service

- Targeted advertising in specific industry publications where you want to create demand
- Sponsorship opportunities at trade conferences or national conferences that provide your company with awareness generates interest in your website and/or sales force to create new sales

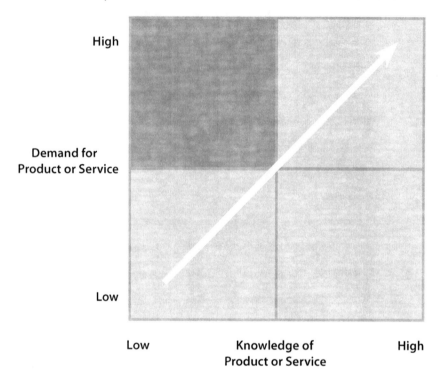

Increasing Demand for product or service: What Type of Marketing Activities Should You Pursue?

Refer to Chart 3 here to review. Chart 3 is for increasing demand.

If you are starting to see an increase in demand for your product or service, this is great news and congratulations! Your product or service is on an uphill swing, and nothing can be better than going in that direction. However, there are some marketing activities that you should be doing. Business may be much better for you right now as your customers begin to increase. However, now is a great time to take a good look at your existing marketing materials to make sure you are clearly communicating your value proposition to your customers.

What are the Best Practices for Marketing Activities for Marketing to a Product or Service with Increasing Demand?

- **Continue to refine and simplify your message to your customers**

   Is your marketing message clear? As you gain customers, it is more important than ever that you make sure your value proposition to your customer segments is clear, concise, and easy to understand. Now that you may be attracting attention within other customer segments, you'll want to consider how you should be marketing to those segments as well.

- **Are you marketing to all of your customer segments?**

   Be sure you are marketing to all of your customer segments as demand for your product or service increases. At the same time, evaluate which segments are gaining the most traction and focus on areas that you want to grow. This is a good time to evaluate your customer segments and see what areas are doing well, which ones aren't and why. Also, if you are finding that your customer segments are growing and they are in various geographical regions, explore the possibility of expanding your marketing activities to more than one region.

- **Leverage partnerships to help you grow your product or service**

   What better way to increase demand for your product or service than to have your partners and trusted customers evangelize your business? Nourish these partnership relationships and have them help you continue to gain traction with existing and potential customers.

Specific examples of marketing activities to consider for increasing demand product or service:

o Joint-Partner marketing activities that can help your business to gain additional exposure, credibility to customer base (such as sponsoring a conference with another company or co-hosting an event with another company)

o Purchase Google key ad words that promote your product or service

o Benchmarking reports that show strong examples of customer satisfaction

o Enhance messaging pieces and documents such as presentations, Website copy, brochures, and all marketing literature

o Refine your value proposition to your customers

o Explore marketing messages to new and existing customer segments

o Expand your marketing efforts to different geographic regions to continue to expand your business

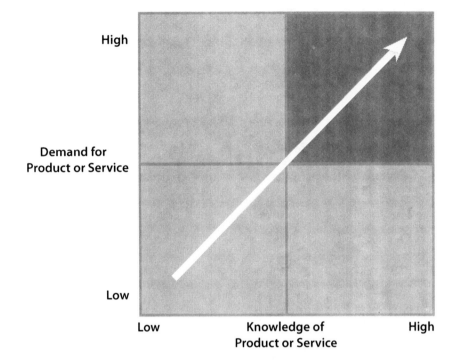

High

Demand for
Product or Service

Low

Low   Knowledge of   High
Product or Service

Strong Demand for product or service: What Type of Marketing Activities Should You Pursue?

Chances are if your product or service is in strong demand, other competitors have tried to jump in on your bandwagon and want to take your customers! If you have a strong demand for your product or service, you will want to pursue activities that strongly differentiate you from your competitors. What makes your product or service better, and how and why does it help add value to your customer's life? What problems can you solve better than can your competitors? We discussed business solutions earlier in the book, and we also evaluated your competitors and what they are and aren't doing. When you begin your marketing activities, remember the strength of your business solutions and what makes you unique. Strong examples that show your differentiation will be key. Examples include showing how your product or service ranks in comparison to similar types of products or services out there on the market.

What are the Best Practices for Marketing Activities with Strong Demand for Product or Service?

- **Demonstrate your expertise to your customers**

    Every way that you can continue to demonstrate the benefits of your product or service will be of great interest to your customers. They will want to know who is their best choice when they compare your company and your competitor. Who is better? They'll want the expert. What can you do to show them you are the expert? Consider reports and surveys that show data points that your customer can relate to and understand. Provide your customers with survey results that show your product is favored in a category whether it be customer service, product development, whatever is going to be extremely helpful. Think about your customer base and what can you do that will make them most interested in your product and why. Show that you are the leader in your industry. Communicate this in all your marketing pieces. Yes, show your leadership!

- **Differentiate who you are from your competitors**

    In this instance, your value will come from what you do differently from your competitors. Customers get confused and end up purchasing a product or service from a competitor because they can't understand the difference. Make it easy for your customer to choose your company! Do this through clear messaging in all of your marketing pieces, and make sure your brand and company name is easy to read and visually appealing to your audience. You need to sell them on what you do best and hit your customers over the head with it again and again and again!

You will want to invest in marketing activities that continue to promote your key messaging, your value proposition and what makes you unique. Make sure that this messaging is reflected in all your outgoing pieces (advertising, web, PR, and any outbound communications).

- **Advocates/Evangelists: Trusted Resource**

When your product or service is in high demand, your competitors may be looking for ways to make your product or service look less attractive and less credible. Advisory boards and representatives are extremely helpful in this case. Make sure you attract advocates who can speak on behalf of what your company is doing and can write about it, document it, and keep it posted on your Website. Consider hiring a consultant, an analyst, or a partner who can serve as your advocate/evangelist or advisory board. This person's job is to make your company look better and more credible! Make sure you select people who are really going to offer you some support and at the same time make your company continue looking even better. Keep these advocates handy for seminars, conferences, and any speaking opportunity that can help you really show that your product or service is a trusted resource. Partnerships are also great for this. Is there someone you can partner with who can provide you a recommendation and at the same time lend credibility to your organization? Remember, it just takes one to two of the right people to give customers a reason to look at your company.

For example, a start-up entered the government sector to sell their technology product. Though they were working with a strong sales team and board, they realized a government professional was needed to help them navigate through the system in the various government organizations. Through a board contact, the company connected with a retired U.S. Air Force general who now serves them as a trusted friend, advisor, and a consultant. Currently, he is working on a white paper and some additional research to direct the sales people where they should best go within the government organization.

Build a Strong Advisory Board/Council

An advisory board/council can help to provide resources that you or your team alone could not enlist. This is a group of people that you would pay to provide input into your business and your product or service. Advisory councils can help you provide feedback on product roadmaps, strategic decisions, and surveys to your customers. They can also provide that "outside perspective" that few people can provide when working in an organization.

Once you establish an advisory board/council, be sure that you nourish these advisory relationships and hold regular meetings to keep them involved in your progress. Or, invite them to attend a special meeting or luncheon to update them on what you are doing with the company. Constant communication about what your business is doing will help you to continue to get good feedback from this group of people.

Specific examples of marketing activities to consider for marketing to a strong demand product or service:

o   Advisory board/council leadership development and endorsement

o   Increased usage of Google ad word campaign capabilities (purchasing more words that ultimately get more customers to your Website)

o   Utilizing advisory board, council member, or evangelist to help write a white paper, craft a testimonial for your Website, or marketing literature or speak on behalf of your product or service

o   Online testimonials for your Website or eNewsletter communication to customers

o   Increased advertising in popular trade publications that clearly distinguishes your value proposition from your competitors

o   Data from customer surveys turned into white papers, report documents that can be posted on your Website or emailed to customers in an eNewsletter, or presentation format or showcased on a teleseminar or Webinar

o   White papers that showcase your product or service in addition to explaining what differentiates you from your competitors

o   Sponsorship of trade conferences, workshops or events

o   Increased marketing activities in all areas (such as Website email campaigns, teleseminars, podcasts, print advertising, various different media such as TV and/or radio, etc.)

Reflection

When you used the marketing demand tool on your business, hopefully you were able to pinpoint an area where your product or service will fit. Regardless of how much your product or service is in demand, there are always ways that you can increase awareness and drive demand. The marketing tactics you select for your marketing plans can help you get to the next level of success at your company. There are a lot of suggested marketing activities, but these activities are designed to give you some ideas as to what types of efforts may help you to gain more attention and demand from customers.

! ——————————————— Reflection Exercise

Where does your product or service fit on the marketing demand tool chart? Look at the marketing activity examples that were suggested for where your product or service fits on the demand tool. Select two or three suggested marketing activities from the area that fits your company. Be sure to include these activities in your marketing plan in the next chapter.

Your Ninety-Day Marketing Plan!

pat yourself on the back; you've done a lot of great work! Your good news is that many of the exercises you've completed will really help you to complete your ninety-day marketing plan. Since you've already done the self-evaluation exercises, you now have a good understanding of what's working well in your business and your core business offering. You now are clear about how your customers perceive your product or service and the value that you bring to them from completing the work in chapters six and seven. After the segmentation exercises in chapter ten, you can identify what customer areas have the potential to grow the fastest. From chapter fourteen, you learned where the majority of your revenues are coming from and what customer areas you are profiting from in addition to your basic customer segmentation. You also have a good understanding of what's happening in the market today in terms of economics and trends that may be adversely affecting or positively impacting your product or service from the trend exercises you completed in chapter 11. In chapter 8, your work revealed what business solutions you offer to your customer along with some concepts around what your competitors are doing and how that information can help you with your own marketing efforts. Based on the marketing demand tool exercises, you may have some good ideas on what types of marketing activities you should pursue and which ones make sense for your business based on the demand for your product or service. Everything you have learned will help you with your marketing plan.

Let's take a closer look at the work you've done and begin summarizing your business. Then, get started on that ninety-day marketing plan for your product or service!

Which Segment to Focus on in Your Marketing Plan

When doing the segmentation exercise, you were able to split out each segment and show percentage of revenues that each was bringing in for your business. Scrutinize each segment and determine which areas you can focus on in the next ninety days and find a way to plan long-term to help balance out the other segment areas of your business.

What I recommend is to take a look at the segments that can offer you the most opportunity today. These are the segments you labeled "2" or "3" back in chapter 10. Some people may determine that the lowest hanging fruit/greatest opportunity segment will be the one that produces the most revenue. Don't be fooled. To market successfully to your customer segments, will need to spend time and energy understanding them better. If you have an opportunity to grow a segment, use your marketing plan in the next ninety days to see if you can do just that. Do your due diligence and get to know and understand that customer segment in depth!

Target Audience

After completing these exercises, you should have a good idea what your target audience looks like and understand who will be buying your product or service. Remember, the decision-makers or buyers may be only a part of the target audience. Who in the target audience do you need to address in the following ninety days, and who is the decision-maker that you need to reach?

Leverage Trends to Help Impact Your Marketing Message

Since you are going to be doing a plan ninety days out, you will have a good understanding of the market today. Business factors may change somewhat in the next thirty days, but the economy most likely won't change that drastically in the next ninety days. However, in the year following your plan, it might. Any type of positive trend you are seeing in the marketplace should be addressed when you communicate to your customers. For example, the environment has played an important part in how companies are marketing their products and services to consumers today. Everyone is talking about "going green" and searching for ways of advertising their products and services to look environmentally friendly.

Favorable Trends for Your Product or Service

Based on the trend exercises you did in chapter 12, do you believe there is a strong need for your product or service today? If recent trends don't show the strong need for your product or service, where do you see the opportunity and why?

What types of favorable trends lead you to believe that your product can do well in the next ninety days? Conversely, what challenging trends are you facing that may mean your marketing efforts could meet with some obstacles? If you've done some research on your product or service, chances are you already have a strong understanding for the types of trends that may impact your marketing efforts. Examples of trends can be reports showing that customers need your product or service or even research that shows that your product or service is in high demand. Use research trends to your advantage in your marketing messages—it will help you!

Is Your Product or Service in Demand and Why?

While customers buy products that they need, sometimes they don't need them—they just want them! The iPod is a perfect example of a product that has taken the consumer market by storm. The look and feel of the iPod has started a cultural trend. Seeing iPods on people walking by in major metro cities such as San Francisco and New York is very common. When a product looks great and when others see people having one, they want one, too. Interestingly enough, if you look at the market research over the past couple of years, people have actually invested more in consumer products than they have in the past four years, so the trend is on an upward swing in terms of purchasing consumer products. Your product or service doesn't have to be as popular as the iPod to be in demand. Using the marketing demand tool was intended to help you to find the type of demand there is for your product or service and has given you some suggestions as to how to do well regardless of where you are in the demand cycle for your product or service.

Marketing Demand Tool — Where Are You Going?

Return to the demand quadrant in chapter 16 and review where you placed yourself on the demand tool quadrant. Based on the demand quadrant, what are the top three marketing activities you think you should pursue in the next ninety days? Hopefully you've picked three marketing activities that you can quickly execute.

Your ninety-Day Marketing Activity Template!

Begin the template by identifying what customer segments you'd like to focus on and grow, and then set a realistic goal for what you think you can begin in the next ninety days. For each section of the marketing activity template, refer to the recommended chapters that are mentioned to review what you have learned. Be certain to do the action items for both thirty and ninety days out. The last part of the template allows you to plug in some realistic goals for marketing tactics that you can pursue based on your marketing demand tool results.

1. Messaging
What Did You Learn?

Review information you learned in chapters 5, 6, and 7 to complete this section of the template.

How do you add value to your customer's life?

What makes your product or service unique?

Looking through the customer lens, where do your customers see value in your product or service?

Action Items: Next ninety Days

What three things can you do in the next ninety days to incorporate all the messages you listed above into your marketing efforts? (For example, place messaging on a Website, brochure, presentation, changing your messaging to your customers, etc.)

1.)

2.)

3.)

Where do you plan to incorporate the new messaging? (For example, do you intend to include on in your Website copy, your presentations, your brochures, etc.)

Action Items: Next Thirty Days

What steps do you need to take in the next thirty days to make sure your customers start hearing about the important messaging you listed out above (e.g., meet with them, send updated communications, make arrangements to change messaging on your Website or your presentation materials, develop a campaign)?

2. Identifying and Segmenting Your Customers and Target Audience

What Did You Learn?

Review information you learned in chapters eight, nine, and ten to complete this section of the template.

What are your customer's critical business issues and concerns and how does your product or service address those issues and concerns?

Describe the profile (approximate age range, expertise, job title or function) of your target audience and what drives them to purchase your product or service:

How do you address your target audience today?

What does your customer wish list look like relative to segmentation?

Which customer is your low-hanging fruit opportunity?

Which customer is your biggest market opportunity?

Action Items: Next ninety Days

What three goals can you set for yourself in the next ninety days to help answer your customer wish list above?

1.)

2.)

3.)

What steps can you take to help you market to your biggest growth opportunity customer?

1.)

2.)

3.)

Action Items: Next Thirty Days

What steps do you need to take in the next thirty days to truly benefit from your low-hanging fruit customer? For example, ask them for a referral to obtain another client, try to up-sell to your existing customer, etc..

What steps do you need to take in the next thirty days to make sure your customers understand the ways that your product or service is addressing their critical business issues and concerns?

3. Growing Your Business, Evaluating Current Trends and Competitors

What have you Learned?

Review the information you found in chapters eleven, twelve, and thirteen to complete this section of the template.

Who is your greatest growth opportunity customer?

What have you already done or created that can be used to help your greatest growth opportunity customer see you and your product or services in a positive light?

List one or two trends or market research pieces of data (found in publications, journals, white papers, news, etc...) that can be converted into marketing pieces to benefit your business:

1.)

2.)

What are your competitors doing well and not doing well with respect to their marketing to customers?

What makes your business stand apart from your competitors?

Action Items: Next ninety Days

In the next ninety days, what types of marketing materials can you create to turn your trends into pieces that will help your business (e.g., taking a trend and including it in a white paper or newsletter or campaign)?

1.)

2.)

What types of marketing materials can you create in the next ninety days to help you better market to your greatest growth-opportunity customer?

1.)

2.)

Action Item: Next Thirty Days

What steps do you need to take in the next thirty days to make your business stand apart from your competitors? How can you differentiate yourself from them, and what types of activities will help you get noticed when a customer is looking for a product or service like yours?

4. Tracking Your Revenues

What Did You Learn?

Review information you learned in chapter fourteen to complete this section of the template.

Which customer segments are increasing in revenues?

Which customer segments are declining in revenues?

Are your quarterly and annual revenues increasing or declining?

What factors are contributing to an increase or decline in your annual and quarterly revenues?

Action Items: Next ninety Days

What percentage growth would you like to see with respect to increasing your revenues within the next six months to a year?

_____%

What types of actions can you take for your business to help you increase revenues in the next ninety days? (For example, hire more resources to sell your product or service, introduce an enhanced product, launch an effective marketing campaign, meet with top customer, etc...)

1.)

2.)

3.)

Action Item: Next Thirty Days

What steps can you take in the next thirty days to help your continued growth of revenues in a particular customer segment?

5. Marketing Tactics and Strategies

What Did You Learn?

Review the information you learned in chapters fifteen and sixteen and complete this section of the template.

What is working well in your business today?

By building on what is working well today, list future potential successes for your business.

By looking at the marketing-demand tool chart, my company is: (Document where you were on the chart: high, increasing, low, etc..)

What two to five marketing activities would you like to pursue based on the suggestions you received in the marketing-demand tool section?

1.)

2.)

3.)

4.)

5.)

Action Items: Next ninety Days

In the next ninety days, what steps can you take using that which is working best in your business to create additional successes for your business?

What three marketing activities (from your marketing-demand tool section) can you begin in the next ninety days?

1.)

2.)

3.)

Action Items: Next Thirty Days

What are one or two new marketing activities that you can realistically start and complete within the next thirty days?

1.)

2.)

Summary Action Plan Notes

Congratulations! Summarize any notes on the action items you've listed out above for your ninety-day marketing plan. A hint: if you use Outlook or an online calendar, document what specific goals you'd like to accomplish for yourself in ninety days and thirty days and post them into your calendar!

Execute and Review Your Progress

Having participated in the exercises found in these pages, chances are you are well on your way to marketing your product or service with a savvy sense of how to reach your customers. You've taken the time to evaluate your business, and you have made the effort to understand your customer's perspective as well as your own. You've also taken the time to really make sense of where you are headed and given thought to what is working well.

Every quarter, I recommend your review of these exercises. This is a way for you to evaluate what's changed and evolved in your business with your product or service. I encourage you to continue evolving your marketing efforts as your business changes. Each time you review your business with these exercises, ask yourself—"Where do I want to be in the next ninety days? And then the next? Am I headed in the right direction based on where I am today and have I considered looking through my customer lens before I make decisions? Have I evaluated the preferences and needs of my target audience customer and do I truly understand the value that my product or service offers the customer?"

Making Smart Marketing Decisions Based on What You Have Learned

Y ou did it! Feel confident that you are now armed with information that will help you to make smart marketing decisions based on what your product or service needs right now. This may change over time, over the next quarter, or the next year, but the work you've done is relevant to what is happening right now. You got through the self-evaluation exercises and a marketing plan template. No doubt you've thought a lot about the different aspects of your business and have learned a lot about what direction you are headed. You've gained a lot of valuable information about your business and about your customers, and you've set up a plan that makes sense for where you are now. Strategically and tactically, you've also gone through a good process for how to set up a good marketing plan for you and your business moving forward.

You've come a long way in thinking about your product or service! Remember, we started the book off in Part one talking about why it's so important to evaluate your business and really take that step "back" to figure out what is happening at a twenty thousand foot level. Now you can see why it's so important to take a step back! You need to have that objective opinion to be able to fill out these exercises and gather this valuable information! You also learned the value of business and marketing plans, and in Part II of the book you were introduced to a series of interactive marketing exercises that got you thinking deeply about your business and where it was headed. And finally, in Part III of the book, you actually developed a strategic and tactical plan for your product or service—something that can be used right away in the next ninety days.

Executing with Ease

So the ninety-day plan is in place. What about the execution part? Well, it's time to get going on that! Part of what makes a good marketer is the ability to execute well to a plan and make sure the activities that are being executed are the right ones. Now that you have a summary of what activities to pursue and you've done the groundbreaking work about where your business is headed, you should feel comfortable getting started on the marketing activities. Remember to keep the customer lens in full view when you execute on these activities. If you are updating your messaging for your target audience, this messaging should be used in all the marketing activities you do. Keep your message consistent, clear and repeat it whenever necessary! Also, once you've chosen your three marketing activities and you've completed a couple of them, try to think ahead and anticipate what marketing activities you can be planning in the next quarter.

Evaluate Your Business as You Evolve

Your business is evolving and changing every day. In addition, your product or service is evolving with your business. Your business will evolve over time and what worked yesterday may not work tomorrow, and that's okay. You've been armed with tools to continually evaluate your business as it grows and changes. Use these exercises as tools to check in on your progress and see what's happening with your customers, your revenues, and your messaging. Pick the exercises that have worked for you and use them over and over again. If you take the time to do this, you should continue to have the right information to make good marketing decisions. Remember to evaluate, stop, look, and listen before you invest in marketing activities!

Anticipate Success for Your Product or Service

Every step you take to make your product or service known better to your customer base is a step in the right direction. And each time you think about your customers' perspective and try to meet their needs with your product or service, you will be making a great leap in the right direction as well. Know that every time you do something in your marketing efforts to make your message more clear and relevant to your customers, you will be doing something that will bring you closer to success and closer to your customers actually purchasing your product or service. Their opinion will always be important in everything you do, and understanding why they value you and what you do will continue to provide you with answers to how you can improve the marketing of your product or service. Listen to them, and watch what is happening out in the market and boldly market who you are and what you do best! Anticipate success every time you make efforts to improve your marketing efforts, and in many cases, you will see that you are achieving success.

Market with Confidence, Market with Information

The more information you can gather before you plan your marketing activities, the better! I hope this book has given you some valuable tools so you can understand your business better and understand what types of marketing activities can make you succeed. I wish you the best of luck in all your marketing endeavors with your product or service. May you continue to be a savvy marketer!

About the Author

SHERRY PRESCOTT-WILLIS has over eighteen years of marketing experience specializing in both consumer and high technology products. She is passionate about helping early and mid-stage companies develop effective marketing strategies and tactics. Her background includes working with small, medium, and enterprise companies to develop effective product marketing, channel, and strategic initiatives that impact the customer and drive revenue. She has a track record of developing successful marketing programs that create results through strategic marketing plans and activities.

Sherry has held analyst, product marketing, and senior management positions at companies such as Brocade Communications, Computer Associates, L'Oreal, and Pfizer in addition to several Silicon Valley start-ups. In 2000, Sherry founded Prescott Marketing: an independent consulting firm focused on start-up and early-stage companies needing strategic and product marketing program development. Past clients have included products in networking, storage, wireless software, education software, spa and wellness, security, healthcare, human resource management, and content management software.

Sherry is a native of Northern California and lives with her husband and family in the San Francisco Bay Area. For the past five years, Sherry has been an active volunteer and Board of Directors member of Women In Consulting (WIC), and served as WIC Vice President from 2005-2007. Sherry has a BA in English from UC Berkeley and an MBA from the University of San Francisco, Masagung Graduate School of Business.

Bonus Offer

WANT TO BECOME A BETTER MARKETER TODAY? Get started with three special bonus exercises that you can download and complete on your own! You will also receive a tip sheet on the "Top 10 business practices that savvy marketers know." These special bonus gifts are available to you today at: www.market-this.org/bonusexercises

Printed in the United States
135320LV00005B/175/P